THE
SHAPING
OF THE
GERMAN NATION

A Historical Analysis

WERNER CONZE

Professor of Modern History, University of Heidelberg

Translated from the German
by
NEVILLE MELLON

GEORGE PRIOR PUBLISHERS

Published in the United Kingdom by
George Prior Publishers
37–41 Bedford Row, London WC1R 4JH

British Library Cataloguing in Publication Data

Conze, Werner
   The shaping of the German nation. – English ed.
   1. Germany – History
   I. Title
   943   DD89

   ISBN 0-86043-109-6

Printed in Great Britain by
Biddles Ltd, Guildford, Surrey

CONTENTS

CONTENTS

AUTHOR'S PREFACE
TO THE ENGLISH EDITION

This book, first published in 1963 and recently revised and brought up to date for a Japanese and now an English edition, is intended to be neither a comprehensive German history nor mere reflections on that history. The intention is rather to view the present-day nation as the "product of history" and thus, by means of the historical method, to make a contribution to the much-discussed question of the individual character of that nation. The specialist will not fail to notice the problems of historiography and political theory that are involved in this presentation. However, in view of the limited scope of the work, detailed comment on controversies and theories has been dispensed with. Instead, preference has been given to the presentation of historical reflections upon the course of national history, with the main stress laid upon historical "crossroads". For the book is intended to be accessible to the non-specialist and to provoke reflection on the German problem, the complexity of which is deeply rooted in history. The author comes to definite conclusions, which aim to be free of prejudice and yet at the same time make no claims to infallibility.

The intention of the select bibliography at the end of the volume is to indicate the variety of published views of the "German Question" as well as to list standard works on German history.

I cannot conclude without adding a special word of thanks to the translator, Mr. Neville Mellon, for his excellent and sympathetic rendering.

Heidelberg, August 1978   *Werner Conze*

PREFACE

Since the collapse of 1945 much has been written, both at home and abroad, about the German nation. Understandably, these writings have been overshadowed by the figure of Hitler, who had claimed that the historical mission of the German nation would be fulfilled through his policies. Hitler's crimes were followed by his fall, whereupon the German Empire collapsed. The wounds of 1945 were painful and deep, but the nation went on living, and German history continued. In the years following 1945 most Germans found it impossible to grasp firmly enough what had happened, and what was still happening, to be able to achieve any sense of security. Much that is contradictory was disseminated about the German nation and German history. It was not merely a case of unsubstantiated opinions. Over the years voices were raised, especially those of historians or philosophers, who – how could it be otherwise? – made no secret of their confusion as men of our nation in this era. Nevertheless, they attempted to apply the scientific disciplines in order to make statements or give interpretations which go beyond mere opinions. Much that is good has been achieved through such attempts. The Germans are engaged in the clarification and definition of their national consciousness in the midst of a quickly changing world. The confusion and dismay of the years immediately after 1945 are a long way behind.

Nevertheless, or perhaps on that very account, there is a widespread need to gain greater insight into what the German nation now is and how it attained its present form in history. The years under Hitler and the wounds of 1945 ostensibly separate us, especially our young people, so profoundly from all earlier German history that it is often difficult to bridge the gap between the distant years of

vii

1933–45 and the present day. But it is not merely a question of bridging this gap, but of fitting the hard years of the Third Reich into their place in German history and of achieving an understanding of our modern nation, taking into account the whole of our history from its origins. The aim of this small volume is to fulfil that task.

It will not be possible to give a chronological narrative of German history. That could hardly be done within such a small space. The main events only will be mentioned in order to aid assessment of their importance in the shaping of the German nation. Only what is essential for the understanding of the present-day German nation will be found in the chapters that follow. Stress will be laid upon the critical times when opportunities were missed and other opportunities became apparent. Inevitably, for if we are not to lose our way in detail in the ebb and flow and diversity of events, the narrative must always concentrate on history in its real sense, that is to say, on events and crises. Comment must not depart from historical fact. Our course through history, in so far as it can be brought to life, however far back the crises may lie, will, therefore, be dispassionate. Its aim is to help to achieve detachment and to liberate us from "historical images" of previous generations, which we now reject. Only thus can we again become familiar with our existence as a nation both in relation to our own history and the world of other nations surrounding us.

At the same time certain questions stand in the foreground. The relationships between unity and diversity, between political nations and mere peoples (in earlier history), the process of democratization and politicization of this people into a modern nation, the boundaries of the nation and its state (or federation), the inner form of the nation in disputes over the constitution of state and society, and last but not least the position of the German nation in Europe and the world. All these questions are interreacting. Their interweaving in the course of history is responsible for the characteristics of the German nation which it holds in common, or in contrast, with its neighbours. It is the task of the historian to interpret those characteristics by means of historical analysis. Vague assertions about a particular national character, whether in the sense of a romantic popular spirit or the suppositions of tendentious modern writings, have no place in our interpretation.

Since this book has for good reason been subject to limitations of size, we have dispensed with discussion of the extensive literature.

A brief selection of important books is given in the bibliography. This contains a small number of general works on German history as a whole, a few outstanding books on the problem of the German nation, some of which have remained worthy of attention in their treatment of the years after 1945, and finally recent writings which underlie certain passages in our narrative and must therefore be named. No attempt at comprehensiveness could be or was made. I should like to thank the authors named in the bibliography as well as my Heidelberg colleague Karl Ferdinand Werner, whose inaugural lecture on the rise of nations in the High Middle Ages, together with stimulating conversations, helped to shape, and corroborated, the first chapter.

Heidelberg, April 1963   *Werner Conze*

I ORIGIN OF THE GERMAN NATION

In modern usage, the word "nation" does not indicate something natural, nor, in Fichte's term, a primeval people (*Urvolk*) defined by ancient bonds of language and blood, but rather a unit that has developed historically. Its people have been forced by particular historical circumstances to belong together and to become politically self-aware. Disraeli's dictum that a nation is "a work of art and time" well expresses the characteristic of a nation as opposed to that of a people, which is not defined by political unity. It is true that both terms are often used in the same sense. But here, only the word "nation" will be used to refer to a political structure and its self-awareness, whatever its form, whether empire or state. The German nation was not, and is not, defined by the sum total of German speakers, but rather by those who understand themselves to be German politically as well as linguistically and culturally. They may belong to a German state or live outside it, but nevertheless they feel an affinity of some sort with the political manifestation of the nation, even if a common state does not exist but is only aspired to or campaigned for by the adherents of the nation. As a creation of history, a nation is not eternal or something existing from time immemorial, but neither can it be changed lightly or arbitrarily; it is rather relatively stable and enduring, even if assimilation by foreigners or absorption into another nation is not only possible but has frequently happened in history, imperceptibly in slow transition or painfully under duress, in more or less conscious submissiveness or in the voluntary search for new territory. If we understand a nation in this sense as a creation of history, language is not a valid criterion for definition, and even membership of a state cannot be an objective indicator, since nations can be divided, held together

1

or joined on to other groups of nations (nationalities) by the erection of frontiers. Only the subjective claim of the individual remains definitive. It is in this sense that Renan's famous statement about a nation being a constantly renewed plebiscite should be understood.

If we take this definition of a nation as the basis for our examination, then the time when the German nation emerged may be fixed, not, of course, in a particular year but in a definite period, the High Middle Ages, beginning in the tenth century.

In the second half of the first millennium *AD*, apart from the final Norman expeditions in England and southern Italy, the migrations of the Germanic peoples had come to an end, and even the Magyars, who had broken in from outside, had been defeated in the tenth century and forced to settle in the Danube basin. Now the areas of habitation in Europe had been determined and the conditions created for peoples with a common military and legal tradition to settle in specific areas. These peoples acquired a sense of solidarity which resulted on the one hand from the personal links of the fighting nobility and on the other from the agricultural community. In the Latin sources of the ninth and tenth centuries they were calles *gentes* or *nationes*. Initially, both these words expressed the importance of a common origin, but this original meaning was soon altered by the definition of country (*terra*) or fatherland (*patria*), so that when men of different origins came together as a result of migration, subjugation, combat or inheritance and were assimilated into a tribe which had a feeling of political solidarity, they could be said to have formed into a *gens* or *natio*. Most of the "nations" mentioned in the ninth- and tenth-century sources may be assumed to have been evolved or settled in this way. Examples of *gentes* or *nationes* of this type around *AD* 900 were the Franks, Bavarians, Alemans, Longobards, Saxons, Thuringians, Frisians, Danes, Lutetians, Serbs, Bohemians (Czechs), Poles, Burgundians, Provençals, Aquitanians, Bretons, Normans. There were not yet Germans, French, Italians and Spaniards. Around *AD* 900 these did not exist; at most they were in the process of formation.

After the turn of the millennium, the process in European history which has continued to the present and has proved to be the most influential in world history has been the way in which these greater nations, unknown at that time, have emerged from the *gentes* or *nationes*, and have from time to time united several of them. As early as *AD* 500, one of the Germanic tribes, the Franks, which had developed during the period of the migration as warlike bands of nobles and peasants under the leadership of a king, had succeeded in creating a large empire by the subjection and absorption of a large number of other tribes. This empire endured, and after a period of decay in the eighth century, it arose again under the Carolingians until it was raised by the coronation of Charlemagne as Roman Emperor to the status of Universal Christian Empire of the West. Thereafter, the emperorship of the Frankish king expressed symbolically the fact that Roman reign over at least the western half of the old Empire had passed in a new Christian form to the Frankish king and people. On the one hand Carolingian sovereign will, resting on Frankish military and agricultural organization, and on the other the spiritual power of the one, universal Christian Church, worked together in the expansionist absorption of the small tribes. It is true that the expansionism appropriate to the Western Church, the unification of the whole of Europe outside the Eastern Church, was not in the realm of the possible. Large areas on the edges of northern and eastern Europe, which had not been converted to Christianity, like Britain and the greater part of the western Mediterranean countries, had remained beyond the reach even of the mighty Charlemagne. And when, after his death, in spite of the Empire's need for unity, the idea of dividing it up as a family inheritance was carried out, the final decision was thereby made that the Universal Christian Empire could never become a reality, even if the emperorship remained attached to a particular family or people. Yet the divisions of the Empire, with brief exceptions, did not go so far that the Empire was dissolved into small kingdoms (*regna*) of the tribes (*gentes* or *nationes*) mentioned above. Rather, towards the end of the ninth century, the Empire remained in two large parts, which together embraced if not the whole empire of Charlemagne, at least the greatest part of it. At first they were designated the West and East Frankish Empires. To the extent that both remained separate and established themselves as empires in their own right, the political structure was provided for the emergence of two new greater nations which were destined to absorb the older *gentes*. Thus in fact, if not yet in name, the French and German greater nations were formed.

In the area which was later Germany, this political unification clearly expressed the prevailing will of those noble leaders of the Bavarians, Swabians, (East) Franks and Saxons who met for the election of the kings in 887 (Arnulf of Carinthia), 911 (Conrad I) and 919 (Henry I). The divided election of 919 is not a sign of division, but the outcome of the struggle of the Bavarians against the Saxons. Arnulf of Bavaria was not willing to abjure his dukedom and sought the *regnum teutonicum* in place of Henry the Saxon. The latter prevailed. He annexed not only the south (Swabia and Bavaria) to his Empire, but also the left bank of the Rhine, Lorraine, which henceforth belonged to the kingdom. Doubtless the powerful policy of unification carried out by Henry I and Otto I (919–72) was a contributory factor when, from the eleventh century on, these tribes were finally included under the general name of Germans (Teutonici or Allemanni); but the decisive condition was almost certainly the desire of the governing nobles of all the tribal dukedoms involved – in contrast to those of West Francia (France) – to further their own interests by political union. Obviously, in the century of their formation, the Germans, seen politically, were a community of the nobles of the tribes named, which remained forced together by the power of the elected kings against all tendencies to drift apart, so that around the year 1000 the process of stabilization in this union was far advanced or even complete.

There are many indications that the common language played a decisive part in this unification into a German kingdom of those tribes which had emerged in the period of migration. True, there was no single "German" language, rather a multiplicity of languages or dialects in the area of Germania, as scholars termed it. But there was a very clear difference between the Germanic vernacular (*theodisca lingua*) and the Latin literary and colloquial languages. Here was a basic dividing element from the Romanic or "French" languages and a no less unifying force for all speakers of *theotisk*, who did not wish to become linguistically romanticized. It is noteworthy that a need for stories, verses and a variety of church writings in the hereditary language made itself apparent, and with it the first movement towards certain standardizations in the written language. The sons of the nobility of all "German" tribes flocked to Fulda, one of the most important spiritual centres. A common language and an awareness of political unity grew accordingly, as noble families extended their horizons, their experience and their influence beyond the frontiers of their country and began to feel not merely Bavarian or Saxon but also (not in contrast) "German". A measure of this development is the gradual change in meaning of the word *theodisk* or *teutisk*, in the sense of popular, to become the political designation of a greater nation, for which in Latin the old tribal name *teutonicus* was used. The *lingua teutonica* was spoken in East Francia, and this language community became the essential basis of the "Empire of the Germans" (*regnum teutonicorum*) when it reached its final form in the eleventh century, even though it was not yet a uniform literary language. But it would be wrong to attribute the Empire and its developing German nation to the community of language alone. The Saxon language, for example, was far closer to the Anglo-Saxon spoken in England than to the Upper German language, and on the other hand Czechs (Boemi), in Bohemia, and Romanic and Slavic tribes from the Alps had already been assimilated into the empire of the Germans in the tenth century.

Thus the Germans emerged from a multiplicity of tribes. In that they resemble the other greater European nations, the French, Italians, Spanish and English, who were similarly gradually developing at that time. For these as well as for the Germans the process of formation of a new nation was by no means complete in the eleventh century; it continued in the succeeding centuries. In the case of the Germans, this development was particularly strengthened by the fact that from the middle of the twelfth until the middle of the fourteenth century all German tribes, first and foremost Saxons, Franks and Thuringians, took part in the great migration to the east, after the Bavarians had already driven their settlements down the Danube and into the Alpine valleys to the south and east. Thus the German nation expanded far into the east, and linguistically too learned to differentiate itself from the Wendish-, i.e. Slavonic-speaking peoples.

To sum up, it may be said that in the period around the turn of the millennium, beginning before and ending after, the German nation emerged in the course of the construction of an empire. This is no retrospective interpretation, rather an observation appropriate to the period. Of course, it must be suitably qualified and shielded from modern misinterpretation. This nation existed only for that small minority of men who were politically and militarily prominent as members of the nobility or who, coming from the same noble families, were educated as clerics or members of an order. Apart from a small number of travelling traders, only men of this rank looked beyond the confines of their community, their district or at most the boundaries of their tribe. Thus, in their origins, the

Germans were a federation of nobility, resting upon a world of peasants, which was only indirectly and hardly yet consciously aware of the first signs of the greater nation that was developing. But even the nobility could by no means be regarded as unequivocally "German". For, of course, again and again the opposite aspiration, for independent existence and exercise of power, resisted the political will for a "German" federation of the great families from the different tribes, as had become clear in the elections since 887. A final qualification must be that the concept of nation was at that time synonymous with that of *gens* and not yet applied to the name German, with its political implications. The combination "German nation" did not become usual until the fifteenth century.

At the time of their origin, the destiny of the Germans was determined for centuries by a great mission that lay outside their realm. This mission was the Christian Universal Empire and the symbolic coronation of the Emperor in Rome. It had been by no means inevitable that the idea of a western empire was conceived in the East Frankish-German part of the former empire of Charlemagne. But it was of significance that in the confusion of Italian power struggles the popes turned to the north, and conversely that the king of the German tribes turned his attention across the Alps to the south; for the Alpine passes were in the hands of the Bavarians and the Swabians, whilst West Francia (France) was cut off from the Alps and therewith from passage to Italy by the interposition of Burgundy. When Otto the Great set out from Augsburg in 961 at the head of a German army and crossed the Brenner to intervene in Italy and had himself crowned Emperor in Rome the following year, it was a fateful event in the history of the developing German nation. For the latter, or more precisely the noble feudal levy of German lords and clerics, were from now on the supports of imperial policy in Italy and Rome. Here the Germans were compelled to sacrifice their bodies and souls in the mission that was constantly held up before them. Meanwhile, they found themselves Germans in "foreign" surroundings which only partly suited them, and were mainly antipathetic. The Universal Empire was never even a generally recognized institution in the west, only an idea which never fully corresponded with reality. Within the limitations of its development it had always to fight for survival. After 961, it was the German nobility who had to carry on this struggle. In doing so, the German ruling class was brought closer together, even if this duty was often regarded as a burden which many tried to abandon. But in the long run the task could not be fulfilled; it was beyond the strength of the Germans. And as the idea of a western Christian empire of German royal families was not even unanimously supported by the German nobility, was widely rejected in Italy, and barely impinged on the developing French nation, the Italian campaigns, which roused the resistance of the Italian towns in spite of strong support from the imperial court in Italy, came in practice to seem more and more like intrusions by one nation into the territory of the other.

Today we are as sceptical of a prevalent nineteenth-century Protestant and national-liberal criticism, that German imperial policy in the High Middle Ages dissipated the strength of the German people instead of applying it consistently to the winning of the East and the formation of a stable German national state, as we are of a Catholic and greater German-federalist view which romantically defended this policy. The Roman policy of the Ottos, Salians and Stauffer has nothing to do with the political manoeuvrings of the nineteenth century. Retrospective denunciations or idealizations of past political decisions are always questionable; they obscure historical understanding and are poor aids to explanation of the actual present. What is beyond mere opinion is that the Italian policy of the German kings in the Middle Ages was an appropriate, even if imperfect, expression of the aspiration for a Christendom visibly united in the world, but that political support for this idea barely went beyond the nobility of the German nation, so that the aim was not achieved. But the tension that resulted from bearing in its name the claim to leadership of a Universal Empire that was Christian, European and "Roman", while it was in practice unable to achieve this Universal Empire, or even unequivocally to desire it, remained a legacy borne by the German nation until the nineteenth century. This tension is expressed in the title "Holy Roman Empire" (*Sacrum Imperium Romanum*), to which was added, from the fifteenth century, the unofficial but widely adopted "of the German Nation". This Empire, in which, in spite of its great expansion under the Ottos, the Salians and the Stauffer, reality never came to correspond with the ideal, was to continue in existence until 1806.

II HOLY ROMAN EMPIRE OF THE
GERMAN NATION

The roots had been put down in the tenth century both for the consolidation of the Germans in their kingdom and for German support for the idea of a renewed Roman Christian Universal Empire. Both, the existing nucleus of a nation in the *regnum teutonicum*, and the imperium that spanned nations, continued to exist in the centuries that followed; they even grew stronger and became constituent powers of a West that was equally shaped by national secession and Christian envelopment. The Germans, as a federation of nobles from the great family dukedoms of the old East Frankish half of the Empire, had been shifted by the successful policy of the Ottos from the fringe to the centre of Europe, not only because their king had become emperor in the West, but also because Christianity, starting out from Rome, had spread beyond the German lands and had created the necessary conditions for the formation of the new Christian nations of the Poles, the Hungarians and the Scandinavian north.

The spiritual and temporal lords, but soon also German-speaking burghers and peasants, participated with extraordinary expenditure and excess of energy not only in the emperors' journeys to Rome but also in the Christian and cultural penetration of the east and north. Cultivation of the land by clearing and ploughing of woodland and intensification of agriculture in the German settlements was advanced into the neighbouring areas to the east, only thinly populated by Slavs. This period of vigorous activity, which came to a series of climaxes in the thirteenth century, was also a time in which the knowledge of belonging to the German nation and thereby being marked, even distinguished, became widespread, and was by

8

no means confined to the imperial aristocracy and their knightly retinue. The first flowering of German national literature around 1200, in which mention is frequently made of Germans as distinct from French or Slavs, of German lands and the German language, together with political and legal documents like the Saxon and German Codes, are a testimony to this early German national consciousness. Walther von der Vogelweide's "German Song", *Ich han lante vil gesehen* (I have seen many lands) is the most famous but by no means the only example. When this poem and similar sentiments of that time are considered, it becomes an untenable view that German national feeling does not appear until the eighteenth or nineteenth century. Of course, around 1200 it is not a question of "national democracy" or of "nationalism" of the masses, but rather of a distinct awareness of being separate from other nations living in other empires and speaking other languages. That is not altogether surprising if we pay due regard to the history of the emerging greater nations since the decline of the Carolingian Empire. The men who, acting together, brought such nations as the French, Germans and Italians into existence, were aware of this as a great event and acknowledged it. For the Germans, for example, the battle with the Hungarians in 955, the Italian campaigns and the expansion to the east, which brought contact with foreigners, were "national" experiences, which have had a deep and lasting effect upon the people. In these cases, the importance of the language was considerable. Written Middle High German, which gained superiority over tribal dialects, was an expression of growing solidarity, albeit still outside the Low German area. However, all those who did not remain settled for life but ventured beyond the narrow confines of their homeland as travelling liege-princes and serving knights, as trading merchants or colonizing burghers and peasants, did this with a shared awareness of being "German". They were united by language and Empire, and far into the east, where their own empire ended and other kingdoms, like those of the Poles or the Hungarians, began, they were Germans not only by descent and language but also, and above all, by the "German Law" (*jus teutonicum*) which they had brought with them and which was assured them as a privilege. Of course not all the ordinary people, whose lives did not extend beyond the marriage and economic groups of a handful of villages and at most, since the twelfth century, of a nearby town, were truly members of a politically conceived German people. Nevertheless, this now extended considerably beyond the narrow circle of imperial aristocracy as it had revealed itself at the election of the king at the beginning (919 and 936). The developing nation was a political community of power and military strength as well as a cultural union based on language, custom, technology and law, especially in the border areas in contact with Slavs and French. First and foremost, however, it was the men who were directly bound to the Empire by status and duty, especially those from all ranks of the nobility and after the late Middle Ages also from the leading burgher families, for whom the great area "from the Tyrol to Bremen" and "from Pressburg to Metz" was a living reality.

At the time when these lines were written, the international empire ruled over from Palermo by the Italian poet-emperor Frederick II was at its greatest extent and in its greatest crisis. The end of that great Stauffer was at the same time the end of any real connection between the German nation and the Christian Universal Empire. This empire had been repeatedly under attack from all sides since the second half of the eleventh century. The first crippling blow was delivered by the reforming papacy of Gregory VII, who disputed the Emperor's claim to be God's steward on earth and instead of the imperial theocracy raised the Church's claim to primacy through its papal head. From this developed a hostile dualism of principle, then the compromise of the Concordat of Worms of 1122, and presently new disputes which threatened the exclusion from political power of one side or the other, at first in Italy and finally in the west as a whole. The result of this great struggle between the last Stauffer and the papacy was that first the emperors, and then also the popes, gave up the battle for universal power. In their place the different system of the emerging European principalities grew up, in which, until the nineteenth century, the struggle was bloodily fought out again and again, between the threat of hegemony and restoration of the balance of power. In the history of the system of European states, whose origins go back to the thirteenth century, although it was not fully formed until the seventeenth century, the Empire and the German nation do continue to exist; but the more the state system developed, the more out of place both the Empire and the German nation became in this European order which held until the modern revolution. However, they both remained within the European system of states, and were even included in the struggle of the powers as the balance swayed to and fro. Thus arose that contradiction characteristic of Germany, namely that the power of the Roman Empire and the German nation, which had still been effective in the High Middle Ages, became more and more ineffective and anachronistic, although it outlived the fall of the Stauffer empire by more than five hundred years, that is, for as long as the old law was respected in the European state system and the "Middle Ages" to that extent survived in the "modern era".

From the thirteenth century on, it was finally decided that the "Roman" Empire could exist only in the abstract and in name, no longer as the leading power in Europe. In opposition were not only the pope but, more significantly, French policy reaching out towards Italy and the growing wilfulness of the Italian city-states. But the dominance of the Empire in Italy faded not least because the nobility of the German nation were no longer prepared to make a common effort for the Emperor in Italy. This was caused not merely by "particularist" selfishness as inevitably revealed by human nature in conditions of this type, but rather it lay in a change in military and economic conditions. In an era of the emergence of mercenary armies, it became more and more wasteful to fight for an objective whose sense and purpose were no longer immediately apparent; and the Emperor could no longer carry out a successful Italian policy without considerable financial resources, which were mostly no longer at his disposal. Even if certain imperial rights in Italy were preserved and were later incorporated into Habsburg military and territorial policy, seen as a whole the Empire was thrown back after the loss of Italy into its German area. Two questions must be asked in connection with this shrinking of the Empire:

1.   Were the frontiers of the Empire from now on, i.e. from the waning of the Middle Ages, identical with those of the German nation?

2.   If this was at least approximately the case, why did Germany not become one empire, which gradually developed, like France, into an increasingly united emergent nation-state?

The answer to the first question may easily be given if we follow the frontiers of the Empire on maps of historical atlases for the period from the fourteenth to the eighteenth centuries. In the west, the imperial frontier from Savoy to Flanders never corresponded with the linguistic frontier. Until the Thirty Years' War it cut deeply into the French-speaking area along its whole length. After 1648 this process was reversed, as France began to intrude into the German-speaking areas, first in Alsace and later in Lorraine. By the late Middle Ages the Low Countries, an old area of the Empire, had in effect broken away as a result of their sea-based economic prosperity and their position between the Empire, France and England. An expression of this was the emergence of their own language based on Low Franconian, while in the rest of the Empire the written language of the Bohemian chancellery at the time of Charles IV, and finally the language of Luther which merged into it, became the standard and gradually penetrated even the Low German areas. When Charles V annexed the Low Countries to the Spanish half of the Empire in the division of the Habsburg lands in 1556, although legally they still loosely belonged to the Empire, the revolt against Spanish rule broke out soon afterwards.

The result of the bloody disorders was the partition of the provinces into the northern Netherlands, which gained their independence and were separated from the Empire *de jure* in 1648, and the southern, Catholic Netherlands which, half Flemish- and half Walloon-speaking, remained under the Spanish crown and, in 1713, still part of the Empire, became Austrian. These Austrian Netherlands and the bishopric of Liège, roughly equivalent to the present-day area of Belgium, were finally detached from the Empire only by the French revolutionary wars. They have never been a High German language-area. In the north the Empire embraced no foreign tongues; on the contrary the Low (as later also High) German language in the Duchy of Schleswig penetrated a land belonging to the Danish crown. The eastern frontier was by no means a German-Polish linguistic frontier. In eastern Silesia the Polish language prevailed, while on the other hand there were numerous German speakers in Poland, especially Greater Poland and East Pomerania. East Pomerania or "Royal" Prussia (incorporated by the Polish crown since 1466), had preserved, mainly in the towns, German customs and language. Danzig was always a German city. Above all, however, it was Prussia, a dukedom since 1525 and united with Brandenburg since 1618, which had remained a German land outside the Empire, even if in the fifteenth and sixteenth centuries the borderlands of the great frontier wilderness had been occupied by Polish-Masurian and Lithuanian settlers. Even the countries of Courland, Livonia and Esthonia, whose upper classes were German, maintained their German language and national privileges after their loss of independence under the crowns of Poland, Sweden and finally, in 1710, Russia. Here "German nation" was preserved and developed in its own "country-states" far away from the Empire.

Bohemia and Moravia had been countries of the Empire since the tenth century. They became a kingdom, and in the fourteenth century, when Charles IV combined the Bohemian crown with the office of Emperor for himself, when the New High German language began in the Prague chancellery, and the first German university was founded in Prague in 1348, they became the heart of the Empire. But these very lands of Bohemia and Moravia, which would later again be at the centre of imperial history, were only German in their border area; elsewhere and for the most part they had been settled by Czechs. Thus here it was not a case of sections merely of other peoples and languages intruding into the Empire, as with the French and the Poles; here an actual nation, small admittedly, but strongly conscious of its identity and largely stripped of its noble ruling class only after the Battle of the White Hill (1620), remained undivided alongside the Germans within the borders of the Empire. The national contrast between the Germans and Czechs had already been strong in the Middle Ages; in the Hussite wars of the fifteenth century it grew to fearful cruelty. But in spite of this, for centuries before and after, the settlement of Germans and Czechs in their common lands of Bohemia and Moravia went on effectively.

In the countries of the Alps, which, with the exception of spiritual principalities, were all united under Habsburg rule towards the end of the Middle Ages, Italians, Ladins and above all Alpine Slavs lived partly divided and partly on the edges of the German area of settlement, so that here the German linguistic frontier did not coincide with that of the Empire.

In addition, from the Middle Ages on, many German language islands were preserved in privileged positions, especially in Transylvania, far from enclosed German territory and the edges of the Empire.

Finally, the Swiss Confederation, which was not a linguistic unity, detached itself by a long process more from the Habsburgs than from the Empire. But as the Habsburgs and the Empire moved closer politically, the move for freedom of the Confederation operated as a separation from the latter; it was finally legally completed in 1648. But in contrast to the Netherlands, the High German community remained preserved here in the German parts of developing Switzerland. Thus, to the present day, in spite of this political separation, the German-speaking Swiss have remained extraordinarily active, innovatory and stimulating in many ways, in scientific and artistic German circles. Nevertheless, the political separation was permanent, and was considerably strengthened in the hearts of the Swiss when the old Empire, with whose neighbouring territories the small political communities of the Confederation had much in common, had finally collapsed in 1806.

The result of our tour along the frontiers is clear. Nowhere did imperial and linguistic frontiers coincide. But the great majority of German speakers nevertheless lived within the Empire, and by far the greatest area of the Empire was settled by Germans. But since the Middle Ages many German-speaking people had been living outside the Empire, especially in the east, and since 1648 also in the west. Conversely, extensive areas of the Empire were inhabited by non-Germans, although the number of French speakers declined ever more rapidly after 1648 as the result of imperial losses of territory.

Strictly speaking, therefore, the imperial frontier did not enclose one German empire. On the other hand, most Germans lived inside, and in general it may be said that non-Germans inside and Germans outside the Empire were so consciously or unconsciously accustomed to this that there was nowhere a "blood-soaked frontier", to use a slogan of the years after 1919, or an "irredenta". The evocation of such terms, which are inappropriate to pre-revolutionary Europe, indicates how remote the older European order was from the destructive struggles for nationhood of the nineteenth and twentieth centuries, although even at that time conflicts between nations or even language-groups, as well as adjustments of older laws of nationality, were not unknown. But these concerned not whole peoples but estates (*Stände*). It was not the mass of subject and serving people that was important here, but only the men who – whether nobles or burghers – were the responsible supports of the "common weal" as "burgher society" or "the political estate". "Nation" was understood in the sense of estate. Properly speaking, the nations of Europe from the fifteenth to the eighteenth century consisted of those men who were represented by members of the imperial or national assemblies, whether in person, like the nobility, or as delegates for their town or sometimes even peasant community. The Voters and members of the English parliament, the French Estates General, and the Swedish and Polish Imperial Diets were at any given time the English, French, Swedish or Polish nation. The same was true of the German nation or the "imperial princes" at the Imperial Diet. But Germany differed from the above examples of other nations in that it was a combination of many states. The princes of these states counted at the Imperial Diet as "imperial princes" alongside imperial counts, imperial abbots and imperial burghers. The individual princedoms of the Empire had their own assemblies of noble and burgher, and even, in a small number of cases, of peasant estates. The consequence was a tendency to form country-states, as the (political) nation found its expression everywhere in Europe in estate assemblies. Yet in face of the imperial nation of the Germans, in spite of certain attempts in this direction, neither in the old Empire nor in the nineteenth century did designations like Bavarian, Würtemburg or Saxon nation take firm hold. Even with the two Greats, Prussia and Austria, this was rarely the case.

If we take into account the distinction between an older, estates-based nation and a modern democratic one, the contention that imperial and linguistic frontiers were never identical begins to lose weight. For it was of little importance whether the countryfolk spoke Polish in Upper Silesia or Wendish in Carinthia and Carniola. What was important was whether the nobility and the leading families in the towns considered themselves of the German nation, or if this was not the case, as for example in Savoy or in individuals of foreign extraction and language still in process of assimilation, whether they were at least loyal to the Empire. Seen in this light the Empire was German to a much greater extent than might have appeared at first sight on examining the frontiers. The frontiers of the German nation coincided with those of the Empire less in language and custom than in the consciousness of those of political and social standing, the "status politicus", rather as the frontiers of the French nation coincided with those of the French monarchy, in spite of all the lack of uniformity of the language areas. The pre-revolutionary national states were the historical precondition for the emergence in the nineteenth century of nation-states in the modern sense. Historical frontiers could then have the effect of developing a national feeling, even linguistically, in all those who lived within these frontiers. The course of the French nation from a monarchy with estates through the Revolution to a nation-state which became democratic is the finest and purest example of this. This comparison leads to the second question posed above, concerning the uniqueness of the formation of the modern state in Germany.

Hegel begins the introduction to his manuscript on the constitution of Germany (1801–2) with the sentence, "Germany is no longer a state". On the criterion as to what first and foremost constitutes a state, Hegel says, "For a mass of people to form a state, it is necessary that they have a common defence force and an executive power". But this had no longer been the case with the Empire, which had no finances and which was forced to rely on the goodwill of the German states in the Diet in order to raise an imperial army in what was an impossibly antiquated and inadequate way. Hegel's observation hit the nail on the head. If imperial military organization and disposable forces had been adequate to requirements under the Saxon, Salian and early Stauffer kings, they had no longer been so since the extension of the Empire into southern Italy in the changing conditions of the thirteenth century. At the very moment when he was over-stretched, however, the Emperor found himself compelled to concede privileges to the German princes spiritual and temporal, especially rights in connection with courts, customs, currency and fortresses, rights which in practice they had already more or less appropriated for themselves as "rulers" (*domini terrae*). With the two laws of 1220 and 1232 in favour of the princes, the first legal steps were taken for the division or dispersal of state power in Germany, a process which reached its peak in the concept of the sovereignty of the princes in the Peace of Westphalia in 1648. From the thirteenth century up till 1806 the Emperor was accorded the dignity of supreme head of a loose, barely effective legal and feudal union. But the larger princedoms were able in the course of time to free themselves entirely from the jurisdiction of the higher imperial courts, and the feudal bond to the Emperor was severed often enough and replaced by counteralliances when princes felt threatened or their interests dictated.

Thus, bound by old laws and visible only in signs and symbols, the Holy Roman Empire of the German Nation continued to exist for centuries as a venerable framework for the shared political life of the Germans. But it had not become a state like France, Spain or

Sweden. Rather did the principalities, as they had taken shape at the time of the Stauffer, develop in the course of the sixteenth, seventeenth and eighteenth centuries within the Empire into modern states with an executive and military organization similar to those of France, Spain or Sweden. The larger ones became states within the European system and thereby often came into conflict with their duty to Emperor and Empire. The Empire faded politically into the background and even if right to the end it was able to play a certain part in the drama of political power in Europe, it was only because at the same time the Roman-German Emperor in Vienna ruled over the land-mass of the Habsburg territories in the south-east and west of the Empire. Frederick the Great wrote in his *History of my Time:* "The German Empire is powerful when one sees its host of kings, electors and princes. It is weak when one considers the rival interests which separate the princes. The Diet of Ratisbon is only a shadow and a pale memory of what it once was. Now it is an assembly of lawyers for whom the form is more than the substance. A minister whom a prince sends to this assembly is like a court dog barking at the moon. If war has to be decided on, the Imperial Court knows how to interweave its private disputes with the interests of the Emperor, in order to use German power as an instrument of its ambitious designs." This was written by the same king who, for the sake of his own ambitious designs, used his power and European alliances as a prince of the Habsburg Empire to seize the province of Silesia, thereby to elevate Prussia to the rank of European power and to inaugurate for over a century the dualism of the two great German powers, Austria and Prussia. For him the Empire was a phantom in face of the "glory of the House of Brandenburg" and the "interests" of the Prussian monarchy. Nevertheless already in the eighteenth century the achievements of the French-speaking and poetry-reading "philosopher on the throne" had caused him to be admired, far beyond the Prussian frontiers, as a great German.

Several serious attempts were made in two directions to restore the Empire from its venerably powerless holiness to an effective form: one by the leading princes, mainly the electors, in the direction of a joint princely "imperial regiment", which would have meant the legitimation for the whole imperial area of the alliance of princes and towns which had repeatedly formed from the thirteenth to the eighteenth century. In the dangerous confusion of the fourteenth and fifteenth centuries, it is not least the policy of the electors which led to a strengthening of the feeling of imperial solidarity and a move to reform the Empire of the "German Nation". All this came to a head in efforts at imperial reform at the time of Maximilian I and Charles V, but it did not reach as far as the establishment of a princely "imperial regiment"; and in the subsequent periods, from the Schmalkaldic League of the years after 1531 until the League of German Princes of 1785, it only survived negatively and defensively in resistance to threatening imperial predominance and for "German liberty". But even then, occasional serious plans for imperial reform had a part to play in the direction of freedom for the imperial states within a German federàtion, as with Leibnitz in 1670 and in the League of German Princes, but especially with Carl August of Weimar in 1785. There were, however, even fewer prospects of its realization in those late years of the Empire than in 1495 or 1521.

Against this idea of the Empire as a League of Princes there were repeated theoretical and practical attempts to strengthen the central power of the Emperor, even to make the Empire a state of absolute imperial power. Charles V and Ferdinand II made the first attempts to achieve this aim in the years round 1550 and 1630, and failed.

On both occasions, with Charles V and Ferdinand II, the dispute over the Empire as imperial monarchy or League of Princes aristo-cracy was sharpened by schism. For the Protestant princes of the Schmalkaldic League, the absolute rule of Charles V was "Spanish servitude". In the concept of "German liberty", evangelical protest against "papal bondage" ran alongside the consciousness of fighting for the old rights and freedoms. The Emperor was feared and opposed not primarily as supreme head of the Empire, but as a Catholic universal monarch who, in the eyes of the Protestant princes, posed a threat to evangelical and estates freedom. Only the equation that German liberty coincided with evangelical freedom did not balance, because both at the time of the Reformation and in the Thirty Years' War Catholic and Protestant princes had formed alliances when it seemed beneficial to oppose papal supremacy. Bavaria, as rival of the Habsburgs and repeatedly allied to France, may be seen as the best example of this.

That the Empire had not become a state is most clearly seen in the settlement of the confessional question arising after Luther's and Zwingli's Reformation. Emperor Charles V, who desired to restore the unity of the old Church, stood against the "Empire", which was manifest at the Diets in the diversity of princely power.

But in this Empire of the princes it was not possible to lead the Catholic or the Protestant alignment to victory; instead there was a compromise, recognition in imperial law of the Lutheran Protestants (1555) and finally also of the Reformed movement (1648), with the principle *Cuius regio, eius religio* very strictly adhered to at first in the individual states. In this, the principalities of the Empire acted as all European states did within their boundaries, often with blood and iron; they compelled confessional unity in their state, whether because as ardent believers they were so convinced of the heresy or the depravity of the other faith that they wished to help their subjects to salvation by force, or because, intending to increase and preserve the power of their state, they regarded it as desirable to remove the weakening division as such. Thus the states of Europe always became either Catholic or Protestant. But the Empire, which was not a state, harboured the two, or three, confessions in the midst of its states and small domains. This can be seen in the way in which in the Diet, in all disputes which touched upon confessional questions or interests, the division of the Diet into the three assemblies of electors, princes and towns gave way to the dual division of an *itio in partes*. In these "parties" (*partes*) of the *corpus catholicorum* and the *corpus evangelicorum* the estates principle was officially broken in favour of a division on lines of faith; here may already be found the beginnings of the later confessional and ideological basis for the foundation of political parties in Germany. Nevertheless, "German Nation" in the sense of pre-revolutionary social order and old German liberty still meant much to Protestant and Catholic alike.

We have seen that the Empire, as measured by modern politics of commercial interest and power, was largely lacking in substance on the eve of the upheaval in Europe due to the French Revolution, if not long before. That it nevertheless existed unmolested even in the seventeenth and eighteenth centuries, was an indication that even in the European state-system of the Age of Enlightenment there was still great respect for the durability of old legal forms, and it was part of the principle of political balance that an old legal title, as the Holy Roman Empire was, should be respected or at least tolerated as a fact of life. It was equally significant that the colourful diversity of tiny communities and domains, which only in a few cases merit the title of "state" in the modern sense, were left comparatively unmolested in political obscurity in the south-west of the Empire and in the Swiss Confederation. It was this very south-west corner of the Empire reaching as far as the clerical domains of the Rhineland that was known in popular parlance as "the Empire". And in fact imperial awareness was more alive in the many small remote areas than elsewhere, especially in the imperial towns, where the symbol of the imperial eagle was to be seen on gates and townhalls. So here the Empire and the German nation were least under pressure from ambitious principalities in which a feeling for their own state was trained and cultivated as loyalty to the monarch. The greater and the more extensive the state was, the larger did it and its ruler loom in the minds of its subjects, and the more the Empire receded out of mind. Nevertheless, we cannot regard awareness of the Empire as extinguished in the medium-sized and larger German states. The Empire, strong in the south-west, weaker in the rest of Germany, seemed, right up to the end, in spite of all its inadequacy and senility, to be the shell in which the German nation was politically housed and felt at home. For most people it had become taken for granted, a reassuring condition of their existence, but for an alert minority of imperial patriots, such as Leibnitz, it was the object of reflection, opinion and acknowledgement.

Something that may not simply be equated with this imperial patriotism is the self-awareness of cultured burghers with regard to German language, literature and art, which had come alive with Humanism and became increasingly widespread in the eighteenth century with the upsurge of national literature. It is true that national political interest and patriotic feeling are in no way lacking in this eighteenth-century literature, and it is very striking that in it a highly fertilizing part was played by towns of the German linguistic or cultural areas outside the then boundaries of the Empire, like Strasbourg, Zurich, Königsberg, Riga and Copenhagen; but it did not happen frequently that patriotic odes were written on the Empire and the attendant German nation, as by Klopstock. The literary eruption in the Germans of those decades was rather a movement for intellectual, philosophical and aesthetic, as well as social, emancipation, to which was joined a popular German protest against French narrowness and domination. However this great movement of the German spirit may not primarily be understood in a political sense. It was of great significance for modern German national consciousness that, although this intellectual "German movement" brought the Germans their classical national literature at that historical period of the secularization of Christian belief, of the Enlightenment, and of the modern revolution, nevertheless, in contrast to France, the path of radical criticism was not taken as far as social and political upheaval. In spite of all its watering-down and reinterpretation, Christian belief remained longer intact, and more effective, in Germany, not only in popular custom but also among the literati and the cultured. In Germany, therefore, the Enlightenment largely lacked the extreme sharpness that it had elsewhere, and the anti-Enlightenment protest movements from Storm and Stress to Romanticism were basically Christian. Their Christianity was initially mainly Protestant and pietist, but later also Catholic; that is to say, Christianity without its dogmatic severity, and experienced as attitude, feeling and conviction.

From then on the new national consciousness was strongly refelt, expressed and preached to the educated in irrational, abstract and religious terms – most clearly in the cases of Herder, Novalis, Schleiermacher and Arndt. However, this was a characteristic of the birth of the German national movement which at first had little bearing on the state and the order of society. At the very time when the German nation was largely politically incapable and then lost its honourably decayed imperial structure in the storms of revolution and the Napoleonic Wars, German poets and thinkers created an "inner fatherland": they discovered the expressiveness and depth of their own language, saw the people who had spoken this language since primitive times as one of the finest branches on the tree of humanity growing into the future, and, without losing their cosmopolitanism, proclaimed their vision of an historical mission of the German people and the German spirit. In the dying years of the Empire, Schiller wrote the fragment "German Greatness", in which he posed the question whether a German could still have self-esteem. "Yes, he may! He has lost the battle, but not what gives him worth. The German Empire and the German nation are two different things."

We have seen that historically this was just not so. The German nation had emerged politically as a greater nation over the smaller *nationes* or *gentes* as a consequence of the formation of the *regnum teutonicorum* and had then since the close of the Middle Ages been as closely connected with the Empire, which was Roman only in name and was German in reality, as the remarkable title "Holy Roman Empire of the German Nation" indicated, and as when it was finally designated the "German Empire" in the more realistic, even if unofficial, usage of the eighteenth century. But Schiller, and many felt the same, was pronouncing the separation of (dying) Empire and (blooming) nation. And this nation of the Germans, so Schiller thought, possessed and developed its "character" and "culture" independently of its political destiny. "Whilst the political Empire sways, that of the spirit has become more solid and more perfect." For Schiller, this spiritual Empire was neither a flight into an aesthetically intellectual compartment in the middle of an evil world, nor a kind of faith in the Empire of God over all human sin and human reason, but the beginning of an upturn in history, in which "naked force should yield to form" and "morality and reason should prevail". The historical mission of the Germans was to stand in the vanguard in this struggle for the victory of morality and reason, but no longer to "conquer by the sword".

When the shell of the unreal and powerless Empire collapsed under the blows of a strong and modern power, there were many for whom, even before, the old Empire had not meant much, and who came to terms with the fact that the German nation in the old sense no longer existed, that the more rational constitutional reforms made by irresistible French power and superiority brought many beneficial changes, and that the Germans would be able to live well in many separated states, which might yet be loosely connected. If that was really so, the idea of a spiritual empire of Germans who were politically only loosely or not at all connected was acceptable to the educated. The Empire was irrevocably gone and could not seriously be wished back into existence. But Germany as a state had not existed in the old Europe; nor was there a German state in the Europe dominated by Napoleon. Did there need to be a German state at all? This question was not asked by most Germans, even the educated, round 1800 or 1810.

But Hegel had asked it in 1802. For him Germany then was no longer a state, but it ought to be a state, and he spoke of a Theseus who must bring about by force the unification of the Germans in a national state. Hegel was not alone in this: not only Machiavelli but many German patriots of the sixteenth to the eighteenth century had repeatedly expressed the idea in much the same way as Friedrich Carl Moser, that the Germans "in inner power and strength [were] the first Empire in Europe", but that this power had been thrown away, so that they were "both a great and a despicable people with the possibility of happiness, but in reality pitiable". The view that the German Empire in the High Middle Ages had been a powerful "state", and the desire for it to become so again under new conditions and by new means, was traditional with imperial patriots, and acquired a new actuality when the old Empire, which had for a long time been recognized as ailing, did in fact collapse. If this idea was to be taken up anew, then the utopian or unreal empire of a spiritual Germany or a mere "culture-nation" was not enough: "Theseus" was needed, and a German national state must be fought for to replace the old Empire. In fact this fight became the content of German history between 1806 and 1866–71.

III NATIONAL MOVEMENT—GERMAN CONFEDERATION

The end of the Empire and the collapse of the European state-system not only occurred at the same time; they were two in a great series of events. Together they destroyed the old system of European polity, which for centuries had been the mainstay of a social order resting on the estates system, and of those nations which had exhibited this order. In its place was created a Europe partly indirectly and partly directly dominated by France, both in its international relations and in its social and political constitution. The way of life which until then had been still largely dominated by the nobility was branded by the revolutionaries as "feudalism" and was to be changed by reforms in favour of effectively centralized state bureaucracies and of a bourgeois society liberated from economic and social fetters. Germany was deeply affected by such reforms, as it was by ruthless boundary changes. Along with Emperor and Empire disappeared everything which had still given meaning to the old constitution and which had especially distinguished the Empire: the imperial towns, counties, demesnes and abbeys, but above all the states of the spiritual princes. In 1803 and 1806 the German princes were given extra territories at the expense of the latter by the grace of Napoleon; in this the question of compensation for lost areas on the left bank of the Rhine played a considerable part. Everywhere the French Empire was extended to the Rhine. Between the latter and the main German states of Austria and Prussia, which remained half-independent, the new enlarged secondary states formed the so-called Confederation of the Rhine. Here, not only were the reforms mentioned above carried out on the French pattern, but by virtue of the Rhine Confederation

Act of 1806 the foundations were laid for a one-sided pact in favour of France, and thus for the subordination of these German lands, militarily and in matters of foreign policy, to the will of Napoleon, their "protector". But after the defeats of 1805 and 1806 Austria and Prussia lost all their western territories and were subjected to such a restrictive peace settlement that they were no longer able to function as free powers and seemed to have been incorporated into the Napoleonic system.

Thus, in both constitutional and international law, there no longer existed any one independent manifestation of the German nation. If we exclude Schleswig-Holstein under the Danish, and western Pomerania under the Swedish crown, the nation was quartered into the Rhenish departments of the Napoleonic empire, the states of the Confederation of the Rhine and the monarchies of Austria and Prussia, which had been pushed eastwards.

The fact has been noted, often in a surprised or accusing tone, that at the time of the demise of the Empire there was so little reaction among the German people, still less in its ruling circles. And in fact there were few expressions of emotion at first, and fewer still of protest. Most people watched events with indifference; many came to terms with the new situation, even sought to turn it to their advantage. This was the case with the princes of the Confederation and their statesmen, with merchants and manufacturers, as far as they benefited from the Napoleonic continental system, and not least with many of the "educated", who saw in the Emperor the tamer of revolution and the bringer of progress for Germany. For seventeen years, since 1789, men of that time had lived with a constantly altering awareness of a fundamental change in European conditions. This change was judged differently according to the viewpoint of the individual. But it was the common experience that the Empire had ceased to have meaning amid the storms of war and revolution. Of what significance then was the official ending? And were not the "tidying-up" of the German map and reforms like the emancipation of the serfs and freedom to carry on a trade a great step out of the "Middle Ages", not only for the great number of those who benefited directly but for all forward-looking people? Such and similar observations made on all sides at the time indicate that the period of French domination in Germany did not by any means lead immediately to a national abhorrence of the oppressor. However, all the attractions of French innovation soon yielded to the burden of military occupation and conscription as well as the offensive conduct of Napoleon and many of his officials. Just as Joseph Görres changed from a convinced "patriot" of Jacobinic revolutionary ideals, who in 1799 still supported the cession of the left bank of the Rhine to France, into a passionate "patriot" in the struggle for German freedom against foreign domination, so between 1806 and 1813 resentment grew against the French and their political system. Thus direct personal experience accelerated a process which, as we have seen, was already in progress without any stimulus from external events: the diffusion and strengthening of national feeling in the people, but especially in the educated middle classes. It is understandable that the will to national resistance became effective in the two large German states. Only there could the thought become reality, but even there not without restrictions. It was significant that in both cases this was seen not merely from the point of view of the Austrian or the Prussian states, but was also understood in a German sense.

It was in this spirit that in Austria a Swabian imperial count, Philipp Stadion, and in Prussia a Rhenish imperial knight, Baron vom Stein, sought to combine the idea of internal reform with the aim of German (national) liberation. However, the Prussian reforms greatly exceeded the Austrian in intensity and extent, and as they were concerned not simply with the adoption of French models but with an independent response to the challenge of the French example, and partly with the continuation of their own tradition of reform from the period before 1806, the years of Prussian reform and its great executants rightly occupy an outstanding place in German national history. In men like Stein, Scharnhorst, Gneisenau, Boyen, Clausewitz, Frey, Süvern, Nicolovius, Fichte, Humboldt, Schön, Niebuhr, Schleiermacher, and also in Hardenberg, who of all these was most firmly rooted in the Enlightenment, the link between the intellectual German movement and political reality was established, and the will was born to make Prussia the power-base of national German resistance to Napoleon. That this small minority of reformers largely succeeded, in the face of all the powers of reaction, became one of the main characteristics of what in the nineteenth century immediately became known as Prussia's "German vocation". Whatever individual reform might be afoot, whether it was emancipation of the serfs, municipal self-government, freedom to carry on a trade, fiscal legislation, Jewish emancipation, the establishment of an army by general conscription, or educational reform of elementary schools, grammar schools and universities, the principles and the attitude were always the same. The nation, seen as both Prussian and German at the same time, was, as had happened in France, to break down the limitations of the estates system and to be enlarged into a responsible, fluid society. The underlying philosophy was that man is ennobled by the public activity of responsible citizens and that schools of all types should lead to true education in the spirit of Pestalozzi, Kant and Wilhelm von Humboldt. An idealistic faith in the education of men, patriots and citizens of the world penetrated all the reformers' activities and through them shaped the beginnings of the modern German nation. At that historical moment its core was very largely a community of like-minded "educated" men.

At first, in 1809, the liberation of Germany seemed to depend upon Austria. "Our cause is Germany's cause. With Austria, Germany was independent and prosperous, only through Austria can Germany be so again", as Archduke Charles's proclamation had it. But the victory of Aspern was not sufficient, and Napoleon was victorious once more at Wagram. The French disaster in Russia was needed fully to arouse the strength of national resistance; and this time, in the spring of 1813, the initiative came from Prussia. The vacillating King Frederick William III yielded to the pressure of the patriots and conceded that in his "Appeal to my People", he was speaking not only of the Prussians but, combined with them, the Germans, so that the rising of the Prussians was seen from the beginning as a national German movement also. The war developed into a coalitional war of European monarchies against the hegemony of Napoleon, and the consequence of the Allies' victory was the restoration of the European state-system. After long negotiations at the Congress of Vienna its boundaries and organization in international law now no longer related to their pre-revolutionary form but were bargained out anew according to the interests of the powers. Prussia regained and strengthened her position in the west of Germany; the two provinces of Rhineland and Westphalia were reconstituted. Thus the ground was laid both for Prussian predominance in northern Germany and for the German "Watch on the Rhine" by the Hohenzollern monarchy. On the other hand, Austria did not return to the Rhine. After the loss of Silesia and the end of the old Empire, this was the third important reason for Austria's beginning to distance herself politically from Germany. Germany as a whole was neither reconstituted as "Empire" nor newly united as a national state, but, in the intersecting lines of least resistance, was sacrificed (to a certain extent) to the multiplicity of German and extra-German state interests and was only brought together in a comparatively loose federation – the German Confederation.

For the flaring German national movement, this was, after French repression, the second great stimulus to reaction against the status quo. The young patriots who had voluntarily gone to war for a Germany that was to be free within and without, but not on behalf of the princes of German semi-states, felt themselves betrayed. For them the campaigns in which young Theodor Körner had given his life for the German nation had not been a war "known to the crowned heads", but a "crusade", a "holy war", as Körner had sung. State unity and constitutional freedom of the nation, that was the ideal to which the national German fighters of 1813 felt committed, an ideal which was further developed by the students among them in the newly refounded Students' Associations after the War of Liberation. Although from 1813 to 1815 they had been only a small minority and of no significance in the conduct of the war, while most Germans now accepted the political decisions without any particular reaction, the patriot spirit of the former developed and later became widespread.

The subsequent national legend of a People's War of Liberation of 1813 in the spirit of Körner's song, "The people rise, now breaks the storm", was certainly not true of the German people as a whole and in all its ranks; but it does properly mark the beginning of the national movement, which from now on grew irresistibly. When, later, in the centenary celebrations of 1913, the line joining the climaxes of national experience was all too easily drawn from 1813 to 1870 and, not much later, on to 1914, this was a falsification of history, even if carried out in good faith; for the line of the national movement first ran straight from 1813 to 1848. That the revolution of that year failed and soon faded in German historical consciousness as a democratic aberration, or only remained distorted in the memory, is one of the harsh misfortunes of the national revolutionary movement, which had found its first, youthfully impetuous and fanatical expression around 1813.

The fateful history of the modern German nation began in the political settlement of 1815, that is to say, in the establishment of the German Confederation, which was guaranteed by international law in the midst of a restored European state-system whose states, under the pressure of the dominant "counter-revolutionary" Metternich, again became "reactionary" in constitutional reality. The festival of students' associations at the Wartburg in 1817, an expression of national and liberal hopes, and the political murder of Kotzebue, who had mocked these hopes, by a member of one of these associations, were followed in 1818 by the Carlsbad decrees against freedom of the universities and of the press. Although the struggle of the national revolutionaries went on, to many it seemed henceforth to be hopeless against the progressively tighter restrictions of the "Metternich system". In such a position, there again seemed a danger for the Germans of a divided view of reality. What then was reality? Was it the loose federation of principalities which was yet united in its suppression of the national German movement, or was it not rather this movement itself, to which must belong the future, against the powers of the past which would only be strong for a time? That was the question facing a nation which moved between the extremes of "patriaemania" (*Vaterländerei*) or "Germanomania" (*Deutschtümelei*), as it was disparagingly expressed in catchwords of the time. Broadly speaking, the alternatives were: *either* the stability of "legitimate" order as a buttress in the internal and external relations of the European states, including the German states, against the dissolution and destruction of the status quo by revolution in any, even national, form, *or* the liberation of men from the fetters of "absolutism" and "feudalism" in the name of a new society within newly constituted nations, that is, unity and freedom for the Germans also. In those years of division between received order and violent action, it was not easy to see meaning in current events and at the same time to have confidence in future German unity. What was clearly easier was either to accept the multiplicity of authorities, which was aided by much romantically tinged literature in the Biedermeier era, or, out of impatience, to make exaggerated protest. The former course was that of the majority of Germans, the latter that of an extremely disunited minority, who were together regarded as a "party of action" (not yet understood in a parliamentary sense). They were all nationalist, whether they were moderate liberals, democrats and "radicals" or, from the forties onwards, even socialists. In many, national feeling mounted to a fanaticism for popular culture and "Germanness" as the highest values of a religiosity that was mainly of this world and still largely in Christian guise, in which all that was national acquired absolute value, and the Germans, as the linguistically and racially "pure" people, in contrast to the "bastardized" French (Arndt), became before all other peoples the agents of a "Christian-Germanic" mission. When that happened, the danger arose of a clash between world-citizenship and national patriotism, and this was later to become a widely prevalent attitude in Germany.

(Later, National Socialism found in this one of its most important aids in the struggle to win over the masses. Such efforts of the National Socialists to find themselves a place in the history of German nationalism and to see themselves as its apogee, were followed after 1945 by the largely ill-executed attempt to establish Hitler's spiritual ancestry and, in doing so, to fit in the rising of 1813 with men like Fichte and Arndt. This is so largely accurate that in fact much of this early period of the modern German national movement, although mainly only indirectly and superficially through the distortions of the Wilhelmine and Weimar periods, flowed into the idealogical make-up of the National Socialists. However, a deeper understanding of German national history since 1806 is not aided by lines of this kind. For the retrospective observer, not only in this question but in general, all too easily succumbs to the danger of losing sight of the particular character of a past era in his hunt for "precursors" of present-day problems and phenomena.)

The years between 1815 and 1848 were full of contrasts. Alongside the national revolutionary movement stood the Biedermeier; alongside radicalism and socialism (from about 1840) stood the order-loving middle classes, who lived unquestioningly in their principalities under the authority of their overlords, objecting only in individual cases, in spite of widespread liberal and German national trends. Thus the thirty-nine German states thrust aside German national unity, and the governments of these states, which had their boundaries altered considerably between 1803 and 1815, were zealous in maintaining in their subjects a love of their state and sovereign, in increasing this love, and above all in arousing it in their new subjects. The map of Germany in 1815 was fundamentally different from that of 1789. If, until that year, a German national awareness of the old kind was to be found in the many small domains and communities, especially in the imperial towns, these had disappeared in the redrawing of frontiers after 1803, and after 1815 they found themselves exposed to the effects of undoubted propaganda for the new nation-states, especially in the new secondary states of southern Germany (Bavaria, Württemberg, Baden and Hesse), which, between 1815 and 1820, had granted their "peoples" constitutions for estates and parliamentary representation, not least because they believed that in this way they could promote the assimilation of new areas which had different historical foundations and, often, a different religion. In these circumstances, the often expressed view that old historical regions and distinct, "developed" areas of small states and middle-class city states had somehow been levelled out by the expansionist German national movement can no longer be maintained. This levelling out had already started as a consequence of Napoleon's alteration of frontiers and the subsequent adjustments of 1815, and had been carried through by the centralizing state bureaucracies of the new secondary states. Amongst these were even four kingdoms: Bavaria, Württemberg, Saxony and Hanover. They all owed this status to Napoleon. However new and untraditional these changes in status and extensions of the frontiers of the German secondary states were, at least the grand duchies of Baden and Hesse could be counted among them, and in all of them was to be found a strong, historically deep-rooted nucleus of both the old territory and the ruling house. Thus the "particularism" of these states, which was so despised by the proponents of national unity, was not simply artificial and newly created, but rather corresponded, at least within this nucleus, to a traditional and popular sense of identity which spread more or less gradually to new parts of the country. Herein lay a possible, and partly realized, tendency for new secondary nation-states of Bavarians, Saxons, Hessians, etc. to emerge, which could feel at one with the German nation when the latter was as loosely arranged as it was in the constitution of 1815, but which could yet come into conflict with the German nation as a whole when the aim was the unification of Germany in one national state. Thus the "German question" was in no way simplified by the removal of political miniatures and the emergence of the secondary states, and it remained an open question whether in future the whole "family of Germans" could in the long run be given such a form that "territorialism and Germanism" could coexist undiminished, as it was formulated in the Bavarian Chamber in 1840.

The stronger the German national movement grew, the more vexatious became the "particularism" of the individual states, the more so as these states, with their princes and their, in this, not altogether acquiescent civil servants, developed a new absolutism which everywhere rested on the "monarchical principle", even in the states which, by virtue of a written constitution, had become constitutional monarchies. Thus the principalities stood in the way not only of national unity but also of the constitutional freedom aspired to by the liberals. The national movement, therefore, whatever flavour it acquired of more moderate liberalism or more democratic republicanism, became the opponent of conservative monarchical forces in a double sense. In the eyes of the princely governments influenced by Metternich, national feeling in the greater German sense was already revolution. In fact, every national movement was directed against the existing system of the German Confederation and therefore tended to be a threat both to the European settlement of 1815 and to the internal and external position of the princely authorities in Germany. The demands for national unity and constitutional political freedom belonged inseparably together. The men of the national movement had to strive for both. This distinguished the Germans from the western European nations, who already had their national states and who enjoyed liberal constitutions, even if these were endangered by unresolved tensions and had not yet attained their definitive form. On a smaller scale, Switzerland had a similar task of combining unity and freedom in a future federal state. This problem was successfully and finally resolved by the Sonderbund War of 1847, whereas the German revolution of 1848 failed, and thus the German question remained open. This fact, before and after 1848, connected the national German problem with the Italian, Polish and Hungarian problems, and from this democrats and socialists, among them Marx and Engels, developed the idea of a Europe of democratic republican nation-states, amongst whom the four peoples named should play a principal part.

The relationship of the German states to the forces for a new society and a united nation before 1848 may be compared to a dam which, assailed by increasingly stronger floods, gradually threatens to overflow or even collapse. From 1830 to 1832 this dam overflowed for the first time in a few places. In the wake of the French July Revolution of 1830 there was unrest and protest. The climax of this was the "Hambach Festival" in the Bavarian Rhenish Palatinate (1832), the first mass political assembly in Germany. Its symbol was the black, red and gold colours which, originally those of a students' association, had become a popular greater German flag. But once more Metternich succeeded in enlarging his dam against the revolutionary flood. By means of resolutions in the Diet and secret conferences, the system of inspection and control in the German states was extended in the years of 1832 to 1835 into all conceivable areas. But the flood could only be held back, not diverted. Unrest grew, not only amongst students and the educated middle class, but also in the nascent crafts and workers movement. Although German journeymen were forbidden to travel abroad, where there were journeymen's unions, the clubs where journeymen and political refugees met constantly increased their numbers, in Switzerland, in France, and in England. Here the idea of social emancipation was allied with that of constitutional political freedom in a united Germany under the black, red and gold symbol. Of course, these unions of journeymen and workers abroad still had a very limited membership. But they were no isolated phenomenon; in their demands they expressed a feeling which was widespread, although concealed, in Germany herself. In the event of a loosening or collapse of the Metternich system, they would be ready for action. And as, from the forties on, certain concessions were made, at least temporarily, in the constitutional practice of a few German states, the voices of liberal or democratic opposition made themselves heard more forcibly in the chambers of constitutional states like Prussia. The ferment grew when after 1845 the material misery of the greatly enlarged lower orders became famine as a consequence of successive bad harvests. In this grave situation, revolution broke out again in France in February 1848. At once the spark crossed to Germany. But this time it would hardly have needed impetus from without. In March 1848 more or less all of Germany was in disorder. Metternich's dams broke. The unresolved German question presented itself in three guises at this hour, when the way seemed open for new solutions: as a question of national unity, of constitutional freedom and of social justice in the sense of a new social order.

IV THE REVOLUTION
OF 1848–9

In March 1848 the victory of the revolution seemed certain. The princes of the individual states, primarily in Austria and in Prussia, gave way to pressure, consented to grant the freedoms demanded, of the press, of unions, of assembly, agreed to the formation of liberal ministries and allowed elections to take place for a general German parliament and then even for their states themselves. By May the National Assembly had opened in the Paulskirche in Frankfurt. The hopes of a nation that was now truly awakened seemed on the point of fulfilment. But, after only a few months, expectations were already fading and in 1849–50 they were finally completely extinguished. The reasons for the failure of the revolution were many and varied. But all recede before the most fundamental and earliest cause, which can be seen in the fact that the Germans, in spite of all their revolutionary fervour, had "stopped before the thrones". The revolution had broken out spontaneously; it had not been prepared for in advance. The liberal leaders were ready to reach an agreement with the princes and their powers of "order", if their constitutional wishes were met; for they feared the historical precedent of a Jacobinical Terror and the unpredictability of a democracy of the masses, stirred up and exploited by those demogogic people's tribunes and agitators who emerged everywhere at the time. A closer analysis of this vague concept of the "masses" would certainly show that, in spite of certain, generally widespread, typical attitudes, they were individually so different in social position, religion, local peculiarities and general political awareness that the majority lacked the capabilities and the stamina to make a radical revolution. Above all they lacked great leaders who could

34

combine the fervour of revolution with the practical eye; and not the least decisive factor was that Germany, in contrast to France, had no central capital in which a revolution could be decided in unity. In short, the German people, with all its diversity, was not in a position, not even among its liberal spokesmen, not to mention in wider circles, to think out logically the idea of a radical revolution. Thus the princely thrones, which could easily have been overthrown in March 1848, survived, and with them, after the breathing-space granted had been used, the mainstays of their power, the civil service and the military. As, on the other hand, the National Assembly in Frankfurt was powerless and thus more and more dependent upon the goodwill of the German principalities, the failure of the revolution was inevitable. In addition, the surrounding European powers had no interest in the formation of a strong, greater German state and adopted a negative or at least temporizing attitude to the experiment of the idealistic and powerless men of the Paulskirche.

Both the hopeful birth and the failure of the revolution of 1848–9 have been of decisive importance for the history and the consciousness of the German nation. This can best be clarified under the three given headings of national unity, constitutional freedom and the social order.

As far as the question of national unification is concerned, the liberals and the democrats were united in their desire for all Germans in central Europe to be brought together in a future empire within nationally just frontiers. How difficult, even impossible, it was, however, to achieve this aim even approximately, was revealed both in theory and in practice in the disputes of the year of revolution, with particular force in the debates of the National Assembly itself. The question was asked in double form: once with regard to the external frontiers of the proposed national state, once with respect to the principalities and city-republics which had not been abolished within the greater German state.

A frontier problem with their own states was unknown to the western European nations. In 1815, although Belgium had to wait until 1831–9, their frontiers had been newly and, it was generally understood, finally confirmed, on the basis of the old lines of the pre-revolutionary era. The fact that different language-groups existed in their states – not only in Switzerland and Belgium but also in France, the Netherlands and Great Britain – was not regarded as prejudicial to the membership of the nation, which was, after all, a nation-state. In all these states, within the given frontiers a process of national democratic integration gradually penetrated all classes of the people. Not so in Germany. As we have seen, the old Empire had not been a national state, and even the frontiers of the German Confederation of 1815 hardly anywhere coincided with linguistic, or even nationally unambiguous frontiers. There could be no question of the frontiers of the German Confederation, like those of France, being so definitive that all men within these frontiers, regardless of language and ethnic origin, would be German by nation or at least on the way to becoming so, whilst on the other hand Germans or German speakers outside the frontiers were included in non-German nation states. Within the German Confederation, Italians lived in the southern Tyrol and Czechs in Bohemia and Moravia. Both refused to belong to the German nation. But outside the Confederation lived many men who were clearly to be regarded as members of the German nation – as in Schleswig and likewise in the Prussian provinces of East Prussia, West Prussia and Posnania, but no longer in Alsace and Lorraine. Since the French Revolution, absorption into the *nation une et indivisible* had been proceeding irresistibly, although not altogether without delays. So in 1848 the nationality of inhabitants of Alsace and Lorraine who were of German origin and language was no longer within the realm of political debate.

It was a different matter with the remaining frontier questions. That the Germans of the three Prussian eastern provinces belonged unequivocally to the nation was to be seen in the fact that they took part in elections to the National Assembly. But what of the Poles in those provinces, especially those in the province of Posnania, which before the Partitions had always been Polish, the historical area of "Great Poland"? In long debates in the National Assembly and violent disputes in this province itself the problem remained unresolved. How, in an era when hot-headed national movements were spreading into ever broader classes of the people could a German and a Polish national state be justly divided off? The claims on both sides overlapped to such an extent that they were mutually exclusive. What was in dispute was whether nationality should be established objectively, above all by language, or subjectively, on the basis of individual decision. In neither one case nor the other were there clear, indisputably correct frontiers, as both peoples had settled cheek by jowl. This became obvious in the attempts to draw a demarcation line between Germans and Poles in the province of Posnania.

In the National Assembly, views on the German-Polish frontier question were very divided. There was a traditionally Prussian view that the Poles as a whole lacked the quality of nationhood in the full sense of the word and that they could therefore, regardless of their language, be Prussian subjects of a Prussian king as a matter of course, and it was of little importance whether they felt either German or Polish. This view was still largely in accordance with the facts in the provinces of East Prussia and Silesia. But it was not true, or only to a limited extent, for the areas newly acquired as a result of the Partition of Poland, especially Posnania; for there the pre-revolutionary aristocratic Polish nation had remained in existence and was already beginning to spread in the consciousness of the Polish people far beyond the aristocracy. Thus the process of assimilation into a sense of identity with the Prussian state or nation which had proceeded as a matter of course in the old provinces did not get properly under way in the province of Posnania, nor, to a certain extent, in West Prussia, and was increasingly retarded by the growing Polish development from an aristocratic into a people's nation. On the contrary, as Prussian state identity merged with German national identity, the old position of a Prussian monarchy with subjects of a different tongue gave way to a struggle between the German and the Polish nation. This became evident as early as 1848 and established itself more and more in the decades after 1871.

In the Paulskirche, the new German national viewpoint was already dominant. At the same time, however, there was a multiplicity of views which lay between two often expressed extremes. One was to the effect that in the springtime of the European peoples the injustice of the Partition of Poland must be made good and that in the settlement of the German-Polish border question both future national states must be granted their rights in such a way that sacrifices could be made in favour of the Poles. The opposing view was that the German nation enjoyed the historical rights of her long-standing cultural mission and that therefore the only considera-tion must be the assertion and strengthening of German influence in the east; a rehabilitation of Poland could, therefore, in no circumstances be considered.

No less difficult was the dispute over Schleswig. Here the struggle for the historical rights of two related countries, Schleswig and

Holstein, against the repeated encroachments of the Danish crown became caught up in a national dispute between Germans and Danes. Both had lived together in these old duchies before the era of the national movement and could not now be neatly severed from each other, if that was what was required. The question was whether the long traditional unity of a country should be sacrificed to the new nationality principle and the country torn apart by a line which could hardly be clearly drawn. Here too could be seen how such new frontier questions affected the whole of Europe when they reached serious proportions. Denmark incorporated Schleswig into the Danish state after this duchy had previously been autonomous and had only been subordinate to the Danish crown. The German Confederation, however, and later the Frankfurt National Assembly, declared the countries of Schleswig and Holstein to be inseparable. The result was war, during which the German national movement was enthusiastically in favour of an undivided and wholly German Schleswig-Holstein. But under pressure from the great European powers, Russia and England, who regardless of all political and ideological differences, were brought together by this interest, Prussia, whose troops were already in Jutland, concluded the truce of Malmö in August 1848, under the terms of which her troops were to withdraw from the duchies of Schleswig and Holstein. The National Assembly protested against the treaty but, being powerless, had to bow to the inevitable.

Basically, conflict with European powers lurked behind all similarly contentious frontier questions. But only in Schleswig-Holstein was there a test-case and it became immediately apparent how pointless it was to assert the national principle against the interests of great powers, for whom the principle was either no longer in question, as in western Europe, or to whom it seemed downright dangerous; this was especially the case with Russia.

Even the Frankfurt National Assembly did not succeed in establishing the principle unambiguously. Paragraph 188 of the imperial constitution stated: "To the non-German-speaking peoples of Germany is granted the right to separate development, namely equality of status of their languages, within their areas, in church matters, education, internal administration and administration of justice." But nothing was said about the nationality of such "peoples". Polish, Danish, Czech, Slovene and Italian speakers were thereby only permitted to live without diminution of their just rights within the frontiers of Germany, where in practice historical boundaries between countries would prove decisive, and not new linguistic or national boundaries. So too in Tyrol and Bohemia and Moravia where, in contrast to Schleswig and Posnania-West Prussia, there were comparatively clear linguistic boundaries. But beyond these given boundaries, apart from the additional eastern Prussian provinces, the demand in Ernst Moritz Arndt's song, that it must be the whole of Germany "as far as the German tongue is heard", could not be realized. For the Germans outside the frontiers, like the Transylvanian Saxons and the Baltic Germans, who had developed some sense of belonging to a nation with both a country and international status but who still lived to some extent a pre-nationalist rural existence, the same guarantees of language and culture would have had to be given by their states as had been granted to speakers of foreign languages by the imperial constitution. Basically, in all these frontier questions two lines of thought crossed and recrossed: firstly that of a national route ("as far as the German tongue is heard") from German-speaking people to German nation and to German state with all its consequences even for historical countries (Bohemia, Tyrol, Schleswig); secondly, acceptance of old, historical frontiers, so that non-Germans who valued their national characteristics, e.g. the Danes in Schleswig, the Italians south of the Salurner Pass and the Czechs in the interior of Bohemia and Moravia, received guarantees, that is, were not to be "germanicized"; then old countries like Bohemia or Tyrol remained undivided, but questions of nationality within the Empire went by the board. In both directions there was material enough for conflict with the surrounding nations already, and even more for the future.

But even more important and more difficult for the goal of national unity of the Germans was the question of relations between the Empire and the individual states in general and Austria in particular. If, in general, the question was only how far the powers of the individual states should be defined in relation to the German federal state, in the particular case of Austria the existence of the imperial Habsburg state itself was called into question. In the extreme case, only those lands belonging to the Habsburg crown which were members of the German Confederation could be accepted into a national German state; it is true that considerable numbers of non-Germans were members, especially Czechs. But what was to happen to the other half of the Habsburg empire, in which the Magyars were striving to achieve their own national state, which would include many non-Magyar-speaking people? The modern principle of the national state and the Austrian imperial state were mutually incompatible. The Germans in Austria were, therefore, faced with the decision whether, for Germany's sake, to renounce greater Austria, where as Germans they played the leading part, or, for Austria's sake, to renounce greater Germany, and this to accede to the division of Germany, i.e. to allow the German national state to shrink from "greater Germany" to "little Germany".

That was the meaning of the "Question to Austria" which was posed in the Paulskirche. It was contained in the first three paragraphs of the draft constitution of the National Assembly: "(1) The German Empire consists of the area of the former German Confederation . . . (2) No part of the German Empire may be united with non-German countries into a state . . . (3) If a German country has the same head of state as a non-German country, then the relationship between both countries is to be arranged according to the principles of a purely personal union."

These phrases, the author of which was the Prussian Protestant historian Johann Gustav Droysen, did indeed suggest the possibility that Austria, for the sake of greater Germany, would dissolve herself into two or several countries under the purely personal union of a Habsburg. But Droysen did not believe in this possibility himself. Thus these three paragraphs intrinsically expressed a renunciation of a greater German national state. This would only have been possible at that time if the revolution inside and outside Germany had brought down the thrones and if Austria had succumbed to the national revolution not only of the Germans but also of at least the Magyars, Poles and Italians. But if Austria remained in existence, then the highest possible aim that remained for the German national movement could only be a little German national state, of which it could be hoped that it would enter into as close relations with Austria as possible. The predominantly Protestant liberal "little Germans" like Dahlmann, Droysen and Beseler pursued this aim with complete dedication. It seemed to them that the loss of Austria was compensated by the fact that a little German empire could be more firmly cemented than a greater German empire, in which the dualism between Hohenzollern and Habsburg would certainly have been a serious burden.

In any case, as the majority of the Paulskirche had rejected the republican course, the King of Prussia must be won by the "little Germans", and the counter-revolutionary forces in Germany and Europe kept so weak that a unified, little German federal state could even come into being. As is well known, all these conditions were not met in 1849. Frederick William spurned the emperor's crown offered to him by the National Assembly, i.e. by the sovereignty of the people, as a "dog collar with which they would chain me to the revolution of 1848". This caused the final collapse of the German National Assembly. And when the Prussian King, advised by the conservative Joseph von Radowitz, on his own account and without the National Assembly, but supported by an Imperial Diet that met in Erfurt in spring 1850, proposed a plan for a smaller "German Empire" under the leadership of Prussia but in a "German Union" with Austria, it was too late. The German secondary states were in opposition; but above all Schwarzenberg, the important Minister President of Austria, who had a vision of a central European federation centred on Vienna, threw the entire weight of his state, newly strengthened by her own and Russian military power, into the successful attempt to thwart the Union plan. The German Confederation was reformed in 1851. From outside, this seemed to be a return to the previous situation. But two factors opposed a mere continuation of the Metternich system of 1815-48: the German national movement, which after the upheaval of 1848 could no longer be fettered, and the fundamentally altered relationship between Prussia and Austria. The question of the political unity of the nation had been posed once and for all in 1848; if it had not been resolved, this could only be a postponement, not a renunciation.

Thus, even if it was not admitted at first, the two great German powers were under pressure from the movement for German unity in a different way from before the Revolution. Even in the Austro-Prussian conflict of 1850, which had led to the verge of war, it had been obvious that the age of peaceful dualism in Germany was over. The German question could no longer be muted by Austria and Prussia together, from now on it must be resolved by either Austria or Prussia in opposition to her rival. That, at any rate, was the main tendency in the decade and a half after 1850. That was the way it was increasingly seen by the Germans themselves at the time. But that meant that both great powers were compelled to address themselves more seriously to Germany than before, and that the German dynamic had to draw into its orbit the clash between the interests of the Prussian and Austrian states which were also in opposition for other reasons. The clearest example of this was Bismarck acting first and foremost as a Prussian statesman.

In the development of a state constitution of Germany and the German states, the Revolution was more than a mere episode of unsuccessful experiment. The enduring effect of the Revolution was above all that Prussia became a constitutional monarchy, that in Austria from then until 1867 the constitutional question was never settled, and that the imperial constitution of 1849, which never came into force, remained alive in men of national and liberal ideals, so that it was able to be taken up again in 1867.

The Prussian constitution of 1850, with the introduction of two chambers and a three-class system of voting, which at that time was entirely in keeping with liberal ideas and was a counter-measure to the democratic unrest of 1848–9, was a precondition for Prussia, after a short period of reaction in the fifties, being able to take up her "German vocation" and gain ground with the liberal middle classes. Thereby a serious obstacle to little German unification under the leadership of Prussia was removed.

Thus, constitutionally also, the years 1850–1 did not simply denote a return to the pre-revolutionary period. In spite of the harsh reaction of the Confederation and most German governments in the fifties, it was now nevertheless clear – as it had not been before the Revolution – that Germany and the German states had finally renounced the absolutist princedom without parliamentary participation, and from now on constitutional monarchy with a strong monarchical executive and highly developed systems of administration and justice, together with parliamentary legislature, generally became the accepted German model – in contrast to the monarchical or republican forms of liberal parliamentary democracy in the west, and to monarchical absolutism in Russia. After the sixties, Austria adopted this German model.

Socially, also, the "failed" revolution had many consequences. Recognition of this is important for the development and shaping of the German nation in the last century, the more so as it has generally had less impact upon historical consciousness than national political and constitutional factors. Let us summarize the essential points. Around 1850 – not directly in connection with the Revolution –

the preconditions were created for the transformation of the Germans into members of a rapidly expanding industrial economy and industrial society. In the forties, the impoverishment of the masses, especially in country areas, had reached its peak as, for various reasons, the population of the lower classes had grown comparatively rapidly for half a century, and, at the same time, rural cottage industries in textiles and iron were no longer able to resist machine-production, mainly from England. But since the same period of the forties, thanks to the construction of railways, increasing creation of capital and growth of industrial enterprises, in conjunction with an upturn in the economy lasting until 1873, the ground was being laid for great economic growth and the "industrial revolution" of German heavy industry, so that from 1850 onwards countless numbers of the rural lower-class and non-inheriting children of peasants flowed into the labour force and the middle-class occupations of the developing industrial system. For many, there opened up new prospects and hopes which had not existed before in the oppressive atmosphere of inescapable "pauperism". In 1848 the weight of this mass poverty had lain heavily on society. But by 1870 the German people could see themselves in the midst of an upward turn in economic conditions. This insight is important for the failure of the Revolution of 1848 and the successful establishment of the Empire in 1871.

In connection with this general wave of social and economic progress, three important results or consequences of the Revolution of 1848 must be picked out: the effect on peasants, on workers and on the middle classes.

It is one of the most important "achievements" of 1848, in the catchword of the time, that in most German states the liberation of the peasantry from duty to their lord of the manor, and also from liability for dues of money, goods and labour, was continued or, better, completed. The process had begun half a century earlier but had mainly stopped half-way, as in Austria and the other southern German states. In Prussia, on the other hand, it had been carried out extensively and intensively by a thorough reorganization of villages between 1798 and 1821, to the advantage both of the lords of the manor and of the peasants. The only exceptions had been those smallholders who were entirely subsisting on their crops; in Prussia, they caught up only in 1850, in so far as they had not become labourers on the larger estates of noblemen and farmers.

Although, in a greater German context, the emancipation of the serfs was only completed under the pressure of the Revolution of 1848, it was, on a local basis, the precondition for the transition of peasants and agriculture into an economy and society of the industrial world, as it was for the freeing of innumerable country-dwellers for the expansion of industry and communications. So in the decades after mid-century, migration over large and small distances within Germany gradually replaced emigration, which, however, only ceased to be of significance following the new great upsurge in the economy in the nineties.

Thus, by removal of old rural ties and the introduction of industrialization, the conditions were created for the German people increasingly to adapt to a new way of life based on technology and industry, and to turn from an agricultural into an industrial society. In doing so, they severed themselves, without plan or intention, from many traditions and thus became far more open to politicization in large masses than before 1848. The new prospects in economic life, the changing environment and disappointed hopes for the unsuccessful revolution with its many illusions all had a sobering effect and contributed to the "realism" of a generation which sought satisfaction in a variety of ways in the development of the economy and which was soon striving after a solution to the still open national question, a solution which was not to be found in an ideal world but through *Realpolitik*, the new catchword of the fifties and sixties.

The young workers' movement had a special place in all these conditions. It formed with remarkable strength as early as 1848, directly after restrictions on unions and assemblies had been removed. Workers' unions were founded in many places in Germany and affiliated themselves to the pan-German "Workers' Brotherhood" with its headquarters in Leipzig. Their political aims were both national and social-democratic. Besides their aims of social co-operation, they demanded that the new German Empire, which was to be based on the law of sovereignty of the people, should guarantee equality of constitutional rights and social justice through the education, prosperity and social recognition of the working class. The leaders of the Workers' Brotherhood, who consisted mainly of craftsmen and had no connection with Marx, put their trust in the "achievements" of the new era, the law newly established by revolution and the readiness of state governments to meet the wishes of craftsmen-workers. But with the failure of the revolution all these hopes were disappointed, and in the course of the years 1850–4 the workers' unions were dissolved. This traumatic experience with the state authorities, who saw only revolution and disorder in the workers' unions, had its effect through the fifties and on till the re-emergence of the workers' movement in 1863. When, after this, the German social democratic movement soon turned away both from the so-called middle-class democrats and from the national middle-class ecstasies of the years when the Empire was founded, it saw itself as being repulsed and, becoming increasingly marxist, it rejected the new national state as a "class society". All this has its roots in the early disappointments of the years 1848 to 1850. The chance of a combination of German monarchy with national and social democracy, which had seemed possible at the beginning, but was even then unreal, was a hope held out by the craftsmen-workers as they organized themselves in 1848-50. When this possibility was finally buried after a new start in the sixties, the precondition was established for the isolation of the workers' movement from the "middle-class" democrats and for the division of the German nation during the Empire into middle-class nationalism and proletarian socialism. In this as in many respects the year 1848 was, even more than we commonly regard it, a year of decision and change.

V KÖNIGGRÄTZ AND SEDAN

We have seen that in 1851 order in the old sense had only seemed to be restored in Germany. In reality, the peaceful dualism of the two great German powers had turned into a hostile one. Austria had gained such a clear ascendancy that Prussia found herself in the position of having to defer to Austria, although she claimed at least equality with the imperial state. The Prussian representative at the Federal Diet in Frankfurt on Main, Otto von Bismarck, eagerly desired to dispute Austria's primacy in Germany.

In 1848–9 it had been confirmed that the existence of Austria was seriously endangered by the Revolution, which, in spite of its failure for the present, held further threats for the future. The decision was, therefore, understandable, though lacking in foresight, to abolish the weakened constitutional framework which had first survived the Revolution and to introduce, at the end of 1851, a strongly centralized and bureaucratic absolutism throughout the imperial state, that is to say, also in Hungary. By this means the nationalist movements for independence or autonomy were to be counteracted by all-pervasive state control, using the unifying German state-language, in order to preserve the integrated state. But resentment against this pressure from above was widespread, especially amongst Magyars, Czechs and Italians, but also amongst liberally-minded Germans. And as Austria by her attitude in the Crimean War forfeited her friendship with Russia, with whose aid the Habsburg monarchy had been saved in 1849, and as, further, Austria had been militarily defeated by the French and the Italians in 1859 and had been forced to cede Milan, "reaction" could not be maintained, and a period of constitutional experiment began internally. After an unavailing attempt to accommodate the historical countries and their diets again in 1861, the decision was once more made for a centralized, unified state, but this time with a central parliament. The election system favoured the Germans, so that Magyars and Czechs objected, and the constitution never came into force *de facto* in the intended sense, and in 1865 it was formally dissolved. This constitution is linked with the name of the minister of state, Anton von Schmerling, who in 1848 had been a delegate and minister of the Frankfurt National Assembly and who was a convinced greater German. This indicates the connection between Austrian constitutional politics of the years after 1861 and the German question. In contrast to the fifties, the course was towards a unified Austrian state with the definite and intentional primacy of the Austrian Germans, and at the same time the attempt was made to link Germany with a German-led unified Austria. It was the only time, apart from 1848, that the Austrian monarchy actively concerned itself with the German question. Liberal, greater German, forces got on the move and tried to find a way out of the vicious circle in which the formation of a greater German national state and the preservation of the unified Austrian imperial state were mutually exclusive.

Thus, with much delay and resistance, a plan for the reform of the constitution of the German Confederation was worked out. The executive of the Confederation was to be strengthened by the formation of a five-headed directorate; to this should be attached a parliament, whose members were to be delegated by the assemblies of the individual German states. The Habsburg emperor at the head should symbolize the connection with the old Empire. The plan was put to the assembly of princes in Frankfurt in 1863. Emperor Franz Joseph, who on his journey from Vienna to Frankfurt had been enthusiastically hailed by the population as the hoped-for emperor of greater Germany, made an opening speech with a concession to Germany which went almost as far as that sober monarch and despiser of all national movements could possibly go. What he offered the German nation was, however, no firmly cemented federal state but rather a federation of states, which in its powers of operation would not greatly have surpassed those of the existing German Confederation, since a unified German policy conducted from Vienna would have met too much opposition, and not from Prussia alone. But there was no question of Austria being able to go further. Therein lay the weakness of this proposal for solving the German problem from Vienna. Also, Emperor Franz Joseph, with his greater-German-minded advisers, did not escape from the fundamental vicious circle in which German Austria had stood since 1848. The Frankfurt assembly of princes will always remain notable in the history of the German nation as the first and last great attempt to make the Austrian Empire a bridge between the old and a new Habsburg emperorship, and thus both to satisfy the German nation and to make their unification in the middle of the continent acceptable to the European powers. But we see that the Vienna government failed on two fronts: in Germany because too few concessions were made to the national movement and too much expected of the Prussian rival, in Austria because the non-German nations demanded their rights and rejected German predominance.

The Austrian designs failed at the very outset because Bismarck, as minister president of Prussia, prevailed upon the king, against the latter's feeling of personal responsibility to the German princely family, to decline to participate in the assembly of the princes. What is more, Bismarck laid down preconditions for Prussian acceptance of the reform plan. Amongst these, the most notable was the demand that the future German Confederation should have "a genuine national assembly directly elected by the whole nation on the basis of population". This was a national revolutionary explosive device directed against Austrian intentions in Germany, but its effect was not altogether convincing at that particular moment, as in the conflict over military reform Bismarck, without regard for the spirit of the constitution, rode rough-shod over the liberal majority in the Prussian house of representatives, thereby arousing the hatred of national Germans who saw in him the worst of all the reactionaries who opposed any political progress. Although Prussia was unable to seize a convincing initiative in the national German movement at this time, she was nevertheless capable of negating Austria's German policy in order to keep the way open for a more favourable moment.

In 1858, when Prince William first took over the regency before becoming king in 1861, Prussia was in a double sense at a decisive turning-point for her German mission; firstly on account of the formation of a new government of a moderate liberal complexion, secondly on account of the quickly planned military reforms. True, these were not moves in the same direction but were temporarily in opposition; for the introduction of the law "concerning obligation to military service" by the conservative war minister, von Roon, led to conflict with the predominantly liberal house of representatives and this marked the end of that "new era" upon which so many hopes had centred, not only in Prussia but in the whole of Germany; so "moral conquests", of which Prince Regent William had spoken in 1858, were hardly possible for some time to come. But Prussia had enjoyed a considerable reputation since the Napoleonic era on account of the free movement in her economy and society as well as her civil and internal administration, both of which were often regarded as exemplary. The more heavily then did the knowledge weigh with many German patriots that a German, even a little German, national state could only be created by Prussia. Even if this fact frequently became obscured, or at the time of the conflict over military reform was regarded as quite out of the question, again and again people waited for Prussia to take the initiative. Thus the "new era", although it was of but short duration, was not forgotten; but above all it was remembered within the German national movement, which began to regain its strength from 1859 onwards, preparing the ground in all German states and beginning to exercise an ever-increasing influence on the authorities of the German states.

The conflict over military reform in Prussia did cut off the path to an alliance between the Prussian monarchy and German liberalism, but it was of decisive importance in allowing Prussia to take up the struggle for primacy in Germany with prospects of success. In 1859, when the possibility had to be considered that all Germany, and thus Prussia, would be drawn into the war between France and Austria, the necessity for reform of the Prussian army had been very evident, and the war minister, von Roon, had been entirely right, as far as the effectiveness of the army was concerned, in calling for an increase in strength of the field army and a reduction of the militia in favour of active troops. But here he touched on the nerve of Boyen's military reform of 1814, which had stressed the intimate relationship between citizen and soldier in the militia. This was a question of principle. The conception of a citizens' army could not be reconciled with that of an army beholden only to the monarch and remote from politics. That in this issue the monarchical state, however vital the argument for military effectiveness might be, returned to conservatism, was not only an indication of the conflict with all political "trends" for "progress" at the time, but also had long-term effects. It contributed to a situation where, in opposition to the spirit of the era of Prussian reform (1807–14), the political and social links between people and army, or, more precisely, between middle class and officer corps, were endangered, and later a life-style and social values were diffused within the officer corps which were described by liberal, democratic and socialist opponents of such an army as symptoms of "militarism". In any assessment of this socio-political aspect of the army dispute, however, it must be stressed that von Roon's and, to a greater extent, Bismarck's intention was not to open up this political rift but rather to provide Prussian policy with the instrument of the most efficient possible army for the coming crises. Prussia had behind her over half a century of peace and unadventurous, even in many respects feeble, foreign policy. Bismarck's intention was consciously to terminate this era and to throw Prussia's greatly enlarged economic and demographic potential into the scales, even militarily, for a more decisive policy with more ambitious aims. Here for him lay the importance of the trial of strength in the army dispute. All this was going on in Prussia while Austria, in continual financial difficulty after the lost war of 1859, cut her budget appreciably and was not therefore at the same level of military preparedness as Prussia.

At the same time as this rapid growth in Prussian power, and especially in the Prussian will to power, the German national movement had been making irresistible progress since 1859 in a variety of forms. The example of Italy and the centenary of Schiller's birth stirred not only educated liberals but also great masses of the urban workers and the lower middle classes. The ensuing era of musical and gymnastic festivals, of speeches and conferences, was the birth-hour of new political organizations: for the German National Union, which linked up•with the "little Germans" of 1849–50, for the opposing Union for German Reform (1862), with its greater German-Austrian leanings, and also for the newly formed Workers' Movement in 1862–3. The unrest was great. All the trends of the Revolution of 1848 reappeared. But the democrats were weakened, as they had lost too many leaders in the emigration after 1848 and, besides, faith in revolutionary miracles of contemporary *Realpolitik* had faded. However, *Realpolitik* meant the implementation of liberal and national aims in conjunction with governments and not against them. Here, of necessity, many eyes turned towards Prussia, especially after the failure of the Austrian attempt in 1863. In the very same year, the impetus was given for the entrance of Prussian policy into the German dispute, from which it did not emerge between then and the foundation of the Empire in 1871. This was, however, by no means forced. It sprang from Bismarck's headstrong desire to determine and change the position of Germany, which he saw as increasingly untenable.

Bismarck did not have a rigid aim. The guideline for his actions was always, and above all, the interests of the Prussian monarchy. But this, unlike his predecessors, he did not see as preservation of the *status quo*, rather as the shifting of the balance in favour of Prussia. This could only and best be achieved in Germany, in so far as German national interests and Prussian reasons of state could be combined, if Prussia forced back Austria and took over the leadership in German affairs. It is in this sense that we must understand Bismarck's observations, made as early as the fifties, that in the long run the German people were Prussia's surest ally and that a vigorous policy of increasing Prussian power also lay in the German interest. Where this general direction would lead, what solutions to frontier and constitutional problems would become possible and whether war with his Austrian rival was inevitable, all this was uncertain for Bismarck. It would be wrong to impute to Bismarck, as the servant of Prussian king and state, the aim from the outset of establishing a German Empire, as did happen in 1871. But it is certain that such a result had for a long time been a possibility within the framework of his actions.

The occasion that enabled Bismarck to lead Prussian policy out of its state of inactivity was the change of sovereign in Denmark and the "Basic Law for Denmark and Schleswig" (1863) passed by the Danish diet, which meant the incorporation of this duchy into the Danish state. The consequence was the huge excitement of public opinion throughout Germany. Bismarck exploited this reaction but failed in its aim, the creation of a secondary German state of Schleswig-Holstein. Instead, he achieved Austria's acceptance of Prussian policy, and both powers delivered a joint ultimatum to Denmark, demanding the repeal of the new Basic Law. There was a war, Prussia and Austria against Denmark, and the result was the acquisition of the duchies. If the two great German powers had thus once more come together for joint action in the greater German interest, nevertheless their rivalry sharpened immediately after this common war, not only in the dispute over Schleswig-Holstein, but in the struggle over their position in Germany. Bismarck did not, however, single-mindedly set out for war with Austria. "Bismarck's policy between the Danish and the Austrian wars may be described as the attempt to employ all possible peaceful means to enlarge Prussian power, to maintain a dialogue with Austria but not to avoid military confrontation if it should prove necessary" (Schieder). In spring 1866, all possible peaceful means seemed to be exhausted for both sides. There was an open quarrel. The German Confederation broke up. Prussia and Austria went to war, the former supported only by minor northern states, the latter in alliance with all the German secondary states, a few central German minor states and the free city of Frankfurt on Main.

Although here, more than in almost any other war, the future shape of the German nation was at stake, it was waged almost everywhere without inner conviction, even largely with abhorrence, by the Germans. It was felt to be a "war of brothers" and at best seen as unavoidable for a settlement of the German question. It was, as Moltke said, "a campaign recognized in the Cabinet as necessary, long intended and calmly prepared", but without popular support. The brilliant strategy of the Chief of the General Staff, von Moltke, and the Prussians' excellent state of readiness, both technically and morally, led surprisingly quickly to victory. The war was decided by a single great battle in Bohemia, at Königgrätz, beside which all other actions pale in significance. Austria was defeated and quickly compelled to conclude peace. After an intense struggle with his king, Bismarck had his way and the Habsburg monarchy departed from the war without any loss; Prussia on the other hand, without respect for monarchical conservative feeling or regal tradition and princely legitimacy, was enlarged by annexation in northern Germany. Not only did Schleswig-Holstein become a Prussian province, but to achieve more secure territorial links between the Brandenburg Prussian heartland and the western provinces of Rhineland and Westphalia, it was conceded that Hanover, the Electorate of Hesse, Nassau and Frankfurt should be incorporated into the Prussian state and transformed into the provinces of Hanover and Hesse-Nassau.

The consequences of the battle of Königgrätz were many and diverse, and became decisive for German history until the First World War, and indeed beyond.

Prussia had gained undisputed mastery of northern Germany beyond her enlarged state boundaries. The southern and central German states she had spared were even more strongly exposed to Prussian influence than before. Austria, however, since a renewal of the old German Confederation was not reconcilable with the victory of Königgrätz, was expelled from Germany. Whilst the unification of the German states was prepared then, and consummated in 1870 by the common victory over France, Austria had to stand aside and was compelled to address herself to the now unavoidable task of reforming her empire. Emperor Franz Joseph rapidly gave way to Hungarian pressure and agreed to the "Compromise", i.e. to the division of the monarchy into a Hungarian half and an Alpine-Bohemian-Galician half which was "nameless" and had to make do with the description, "kingdoms and countries represented in the Imperial Diet". Within this half Galicia received a certain degree of autonomy and was consigned to the Poles, while the Czechs failed to achieve an equivalent position in Bohemia and Moravia, so that they belonged amongst the permanently discontented opposition in the Vienna Diet. The further the franchise for this parliament was extended, until in 1907 it became universal and equal, the smaller within it became the proportion of Germans, who at the beginning had had an absolute majority in this parliament of the western half of the Empire, and the more inhibiting became the disruptive tactics and obstruction of the Czechs, with whom no satisfactory *modus vivendi* could be achieved in the countries of Bohemia and Moravia until the world war – in spite of the Moravian Compromise of 1905. Thus the Germans in the western half of the Empire felt themselves increasingly threatened in the course of the decades. They were excluded from Germany for as long as the Habsburg monarchy continued in existence. In this monarchy, however, they lost more and more of their earlier predominance as a result of the extended franchise and a state administration which was assigned to the other nationalities, especially the Poles. It was no wonder in these circumstances that the idea of a greater Germany with the black, red and gold flag as its symbol remained alive in the decades after 1867, even if the various parties, particularly the Christian Socialists and the soon rapidly growing Social Democrats based their policy not on a future dissolution of the Habsburg empire but rather on its continued unity. The party of "Pan-Germans" was only a small minority; yet hopes of an amalgamation with the German Empire extended far beyond their ranks, at least as a general idea. Whereas in the Prussian north Königgrätz was soon linked into the triumphal chain of Bismarck's and Moltke's great successes, which had led to the foundation of the Empire in 1871 and had become an honourable page in the annals of the Prussian army fighting for the German cause, for the Germans of Austria it remained a painful thorn in their consciousness. Along with many others, Grillparzer gave vent to this feeling when he cried to the north German victors, "You believe you have given birth to an empire, but you have only destroyed a people." It is hardly surprising that popular national ideas, strengthened by an increasingly defensive attitude, found support amongst the Austrian Germans. (Hitler grew up in such an environment and formed his political "philosophy" from experiences and events in the later days of the Habsburg Empire.) That too was a consequence of the result of Königgrätz.

In spite of all its crises and the widespread discontent of many nationalities, not least of the Germans, it must not be forgotten on the other hand that the Habsburg monarchy was an "institution which deprived ten million Germans of membership of the Empire in order to neutralize politically thirty million non-Germans", or in other words that the existence of Austria-Hungary prevented the dissolution of central Europe into small national states, and that long continuity of administrative practice was successful to an astonishing extent in enabling so many people to live together right to the end in an international empire. Alongside the "modern" inclination for multiracial empires to break down into nations, the tendency, still very much with us, to adhere to the status quo, remained to the end. After 1871, Bismarck saw in Austria-Hungary a valuable bulwark against the revolution that threatened Europe with its combination of national and social aims, and for this reason he rejected a possible dissolution of the Danube monarchy with the object of annexing its German areas to his Empire. But however impressive this piece of Old Europe may appear in the middle of fully formed or developing national states, even in retrospect, it nevertheless cannot be denied that it was an empire that was condemned to die, because it stood in the way of the national democratic movement that was now unstoppable throughout Europe.

How different matters were in the area of Germany that had become part of the Prussian state, or its area of influence, as a result of Königgrätz! Here the prospect had opened up that Bismarck's Prussian policy could at the same time become a national policy in the little German sense; and the links with social movements of the period seemed to be made more effectively than before, since both the majority of the liberals and Bismarck had the serious intention of making peace after the great success of 1866. The newly formed National Liberal Party, under the leadership of Rudolf von Bennigsen, a Hanoverian, came to terms with Bismarck and the Prussian state for the sake of the national German aim, and, as a result, in the years between the wars of 1866 and 1870 Bismarckian policy was combined with the authoritative social powers of the German states outside the frontiers of Prussia. This, together with the attitude of the German princes, was the decisive precondition for the foundation of the future little German Empire.

The steps towards the foundation of the Empire were, first, the formation of the North German Confederation, in which Prussia joined a federation of all the north and central German states; next, the parliament of this confederation, which proposed and accepted the constitution as a compromise between Bismarck and the National Liberals; then the secret defensive and offensive alliances with the southern German states, and the new Zollverein treaties with these states; and finally the concerted national war of the Germans against France, which led to victory and the proclamation of the new German Empire.

After union with the southern German states in 1871, the constitution of the North German Confederation of 1867 was extended to the Empire. It remained in force essentially unaltered until 1918. If we would seek fairly to judge its significance for the nation and the young national state, we must not transfer the constitutional tensions of the later period of William II over to the years around 1870. At the time of its creation, the imperial constitution of 1867–71 was entirely appropriate for the internal and external situation of Germany. It was not a logical and systematic construction in which unifying political principles were realized, but rather the personal creation of Bismarck, who formulated the constitution after cautious calculation, particularly with regard to the princes, but so adapted it to his own needs – particularly in the prominence given to the position of Chancellor – that he could not be seriously constrained either by an imperial cabinet working as a unit (this did not exist), or by the *Reichstag*, which had no influence upon the appointment or dismissal of the Chancellor. This certainly had its advantages in the different situation following the war with Austria, when the need was to counter the dangers from without, and the various currents of resistance within Germany, whether from the particularism of the princes or from the political parties to the right and the left of the National Liberals. But it also contained serious dangers for the future in the situation that on the one hand democratic, universal and equal suffrage of men over twenty-five had been granted for the German *Reichstag*, whereas on the other, in common with the Federal Council, it had been accorded only powers of legislation, including budget control, but no share in the formation of the government. This, incidentally, was the exact opposite of the arrangement in the newly founded Italian national state, since in Italy the suffrage was at first still tied to a voting-list based on property and education, but the parliament elected in this way determined the formation of the government by its current majority. In 1863 and 1866 Bismarck had already utilized the demand for universal and equal suffrage as a national revolutionary device against Austria's German policy and the German Confederation, and at the same time – in conjunction with Lassalle – had considered introducing it against the liberals, the party of progress, in Prussia. He hoped to strengthen his position in the North German Federation and in the new Empire by the mobilization of the royalist masses in the elections. The enfranchisement of the masses was intended to counterbalance the liberal tendencies of the constitutionally demanding middle classes, although the National Liberals were his allies in the years of the founding of the Empire. Universal suffrage was to constitute an appeal for assent and loyalty, for trust in the monarchical authorities and the conduct of the Empire by the Chancellor, and thus indirectly to help to thwart the liberal desire for full parliamentarism of Chancellor and government. It was characteristic of this attitude that Bismarck, partly out of regard for the princes, who were essential to his designs, and partly out of private conviction, was concerned not to permit his "revolution from above", which he had carried out in 1866, to be succeeded by a revolution from below, nor in 1870–1 to allow the "people" or parliamentarians, whether by direct democracy or by the co-operation of the North German parliament, to become collaborators or independent partners in the formation of the Empire. It is true that in December 1870 William I met a deputation from the *Reichstag* –

led by Eduard Simson, of Königsberg, one of the great Jews of the German nation, who had already offered Frederick William IV the German imperial crown at the behest of the National Assembly in 1849 – to receive the request of parliament that he should accept the emperorship. But it was not intended to be a crown by grace of the people, and their representatives were excluded from all further events. They were even excluded from his proclamation in the Hall of Mirrors at Versailles, where princes, generals and soldiers had assembled to raise a cheer for Emperor William I, as he reluctantly assumed his new title, and the flag of the young Empire was raised over the palace of Louis XIV.

Because of William I and the German princes, it could no longer be the black, red and gold flag of the national revolutionary movement and the revolution of 1848. Instead, the black, white and red colours were to symbolize the link between Prussia and the Hanseatic League. The break with the greater German and the democratic tradition of 1848 was visibly marked. The new empire had emerged from the unanimous will of the German princes, but not from a national assembly. As such, it had no roots. Rather were these to be found in the kingdom of the Prussian monarchy of the House of Hohenzollern. Little wonder then that from then on a view of history emerged ever more strongly, in which the new Germany was seen as a continuation of the history of Brandenburg Prussia. All else merged into the background. William I remained King of Prussia as the dominant state. In the Federal Council he was the *primus inter pares* of all the princes who had formed the "eternal union" which bore "the name of German Empire", as the preamble to the constitution put it. Paragraph 11 of the constitution continued: "The presidency of the Confederation belongs to the King of Prussia, who bears the title of German Emperor." Besides the twin organs of Federal Council and presidency, there was a third organ which was the only one that bore the Empire in its name: the *Reichstag*. But the Emperor, as incumbent of the presidency, together with his appointee the Chancellor and his secretaries of state, was completely independent of the Reichstag. Thus the Emperor was not a constitutional but a federal monarch (E. Kaufmann).

The Empire impinged upon the consciousness of the Germans, who still identified themselves according to their individual state (Prussians, Bavarians, Saxons, etc.), but who were to be uniformly described throughout the Empire as *Inländer*, in two forms: in the

Emperor and in the Reichstag, i.e. in the traditional monarchical sense as an unquestionable authority, above all parties, and in the democratic sense as the manifestation of a nation of citizens, whose diversity of aspirations should receive due consideration in the legislative work of the peoples' assembly. Thus from the beginning the problem facing the young Empire was that later expressed in the title of a widely disseminated publication by Friedrich Naumann, *Democracy and Emperorship*.

Both these conceptions were highly dubious, both in themselves and in connection with each other. In the case of the emperorship, this can be seen at the very moment of its creation. As is well known, not only did William I not desire the crown but he actually resisted it until immediately before the proclamation in Versailles on 18 January 1871, the same day as the coronation of the King of Prussia in 1701. When the possibility of emperorship was first mentioned in 1867, King William had found it a repulsive idea "to see the solid splendour of the royal crown of Prussia pale before the newly polished crown of the German Empire". Only reluctantly did he finally bow to the inevitable, whereas his son, Crown Prince Frederick William, later William III, with greater historical imagination, summoned up the old Crown of the Holy Roman Empire of the German Nation and wanted to see the new Empire follow in that tradition. He had seriously thought of arranging the coronation for Christmas Day, 1070 years after the coronation of Charlemagne in Rome, and for the old crown and imperial insignia to be handed over from Vienna. Nothing came of all this, however, because William I and Bismarck had no time for such political romanticism, which could only have had an adverse effect on the southern German princes as well as the Habsburgs. But even if this was not taken seriously, it was indisputable that now, in 1871 just as in 1848, the re-creation of the title of Emperor necessarily signified a link-up with the Empire that had ended in 1806. But much of this was questionable. For the old imperial capital had been Vienna, the old Emperor had been Catholic and by tradition loyal to Rome to the end; and finally he had been Emperor of the whole nation. But now it was an empire without this tradition, which could only be taken up in a modern, national reinterpretation; more, it had a Protestant Emperor, alienated from Rome, at the head of a newly formed national state, which did not encompass a large part of the German nation. Did not this empire, it was asked, have more in common with the fallen Second Empire of the French than with the universal tradition of the Holy Roman Empire? But this very interpretation was to be avoided, and thus a view of German history was required which linked a high estimation of the medieval empire of the Ottos, Salians and Stauffers with the rise of Brandenburg Prussia in the centuries when the Empire was decaying. Much of the wealth of German history in relation to the Habsburgs and Austria was lost to general historical awareness and to school history books, devalued or thrust into the background. In 1871 it was an open question how far the new Empire of the Hohenzollerns would succeed in rooting itself in the consciousness of the Germans and their environment, so that it could strengthen and build up its own tradition.

This question was closely connected with that of democracy. In the Reichstag, with universal and equal suffrage, an important piece of modern democracy had been built into the Empire *de jure*. This was clearly a link with the 1848 Revolution, which, as we have seen, had otherwise been repressed in the general consciousness, in so far as it had been greater German and democratic. In the eyes of the founders of the new Empire, this was an indication at one and the same time that both the greater German and the democratic aims were now disposed of, or else they were seen as a menace to the political order which was to surround the new Empire and within which it was to fit into the European state system. The circle which the politicians of the young German Empire entered may be described in these terms: now that the Reichstag had been created with democratic suffrage, if in the long term there were a delay or halt to strengthening the constitution in the direction of parliamentary democracy, the Empire must run the risk of coming into conflict with the democratic movement and thus of endangering its own existence. But if it gave way constitutionally to the democratic movement, this could have unpleasant repercussions for the Habsburg monarchy, which internally, as well as externally and militarily, had drawn strength from the fact that the breach of Königgrätz had been covered over by the alliance of two great *conservative*, anti-democratic empires. Democratization of any kind, in spite of the well-intentioned programme of the Austrian Social Democrats from 1899, meant, in effect, increased risk of the dissolution of the monarchy into national democracies; and for the Germans of Austria the only logical consequence of this could be a return to the ideals of 1848 – greater Germany and democracy.

Bismarck's will was set against this. His famous saying that the German Empire was "satiated" after 1871 was meant in the sense that the young Empire, whose establishment after three victorious wars had meant the upheaval of Europe, should now peacefully settle down after this upheaval within the European system, which had altered in Germany's favour, without any further changes of frontier. But from this followed above all that Austria-Hungary must survive, and that accordingly any greater German, i.e. national revolutionary, movement in the German Empire and in Austria was highly undesirable.

Whereas Bismarck had achieved this pacification of the old rival of 1866, the prospects for a long-term easing of tension with France were not equally favourable. This proved to have fateful consequences for the history and the political awareness of the German nation after 1871. The war of 1866 had been a painful war of brothers, and the Austrian "brother" had consciously been treated with consideration, so that the alliance of the two emperors could begin at once. In 1870, however, a war had been fought which both Germans and French regarded as a national war. Moltke's great victory at Sedan and the final defeat of France, even after the outbreak of civil war, were a national triumph for the Germans and a national wound for the French. On both sides, this was stored up in the memory and continually kept alive. For the Germans of the new Empire, it was the memory of a great shared achievement which was rightly regarded as the precondition for the successful foundation of a national state under the emperorship of the Hohenzollerns. For the French, however, the experience of 1870–1 resulted in a desire for reparation, and with many Frenchmen this desire continued to grow into the hope of "satisfaction". Every year the Germans celebrated the anniversary of Sedan, on 2 September, as a national holiday. This was understandable, as Sedan had in fact brought about the decisive historical moment for the German nation; but herein lay a danger of arrogance, of offending the neighbouring nation, of nationalist nonsense in the arrangements for the celebrations and an over-estimation of the military in politics and history. What the effect of the celebrations of Sedan must have been on the French need not be underlined. It was inevitable that Sedan Day should each year reopen old wounds which needed to heal. In this atmosphere the *idée fixe* of the French and Germans as "hereditary enemies" gained ground, even if it was rejected by many sensible men on both sides. Thus the great event of 1871 had a fateful legacy, as German unification in the new Empire at the same time spelt humiliation for the French nation.

This gulf between the French and the German nations was widened still further between 1871 and 1917 by the question of the areas ceded by France without a plebiscite and which were incorporated into the German Empire as "the imperial province of Alsace-Lorraine". Bismarck had taken up the idea of annexing these countries for reasons of military security soon after the beginning of the war and had ensured that "public opinion" was suitably prepared. In Germany the idea was received in two conflicting ways. But predominantly it suited the national feelings of the victorious nation to remember, with a wave of emotion, the indisputable fact that this was old imperial land that had been torn away from the Empire since the seventeenth century by dubious and entirely illegal means, and that, what was more, with the exception of the area round Metz the people of Alsace and Lorraine were of Alemannic and Franconian origin and spoke German, except where as educated men they used French. Such – honestly argued – views therefore sought popular national justification. Whether a country should be part of Germany was a question of language, origin and history. The French opposed this idea with their own conception of a nation as a community of political will and stressed the equally indisputable fact that the original Germans in the old, lost areas of the Empire had gradually come both to feel and declare themselves members of the French nation. A plebiscite at that time would clearly have shown this. But this was refused. For the French it therefore followed that restitution must one day be sought for the injustice of 1871. Alsace-Lorraine remained the bone of contention between Germany and France between 1871 and 1918. It also remained a sore point in the internal and foreign policies of the German Empire in this period. Until the First World War, it was possible neither to persuade the inhabitants of Alsace and Lorraine freely to acknowledge their membership of the German nation nor to assimilate them. The Reichstag deputies of the "imperial province" mainly devoted themselves throughout the period between the two wars to "protest". Serious errors of popular psychology were made on the German side, although it must not be overlooked that the process of habituation to German conditions was making progress when all this was interrupted by the world war. However effective the powers of attraction and repulsion were in Alsace-Lorraine between 1871 and 1914, it remains certain that Alsace-Lorraine was the greatest obstacle to the healing of Franco-German national enmity. But this enmity was one of the heaviest burdens of Europe as a whole and of the young German nation-state in particular.

VI THE NEW EMPIRE

"Where at my age can a new purpose be found for the rest of life?"
These words of the national liberal historian, Heinrich von Sybel,
who completed his life's work twenty years after the foundation of
the Empire with his great portrayal of *The Foundation of the German
Empire by William I*, have justly become famous. For they express the
mood of those German liberals who had opted for the little German
solution after the failure of the attempt to establish an empire in
1848 and had allowed themselves to be convinced by Bismarck's
success. The powerful national state, free of the burden of the
Austrian question, had at last become realized through Bismarck's
daring policies and Moltke's superior military strategy. The
imperial constitution allowed plenty of scope for liberal aims, as was
soon to be seen in the seventies in the framing of basic imperial law,
when the National Liberal Party, as the majority party, dominated
the first Reichstag of 1871. What a turn of events had taken place
within so few years! The aspiration of two generations seemed
fulfilled. The aim was achieved. If this widespread mood of the time
is taken in conjunction with Bismarck's conviction of a "satiated"
Empire, one can, in accord with the opinion of many in 1871,
regard the foundation of the Empire in this year as a conclusion and
a fulfilment after decades of action and discontent. Such a view was
understandable after all that had gone before. It gave men a feeling
of great security, and this feeling had its effect on the ensuing
generation, which lacked Bismarck's alert awareness of the fragility
of the young imperial edifice against the developing power of the
Wilhelmine state. Thus the arch stretches from 1871, the year of
satisfaction in final achievement, to the "world of security", as the
novelist, Stefan Zweig, in his memoirs, called the years before 1914.

But by 1918 at the latest it was generally evident that this view had not entirely corresponded with reality, and that the Empire in which the majority of men had felt "safe" had, long before 1918, even from the beginning, had deep cracks in its structure, which goes some way towards correcting the image of a satisfied, secure, or even unanimous, nation within its national state.

Was the Empire a national state at all? According to its claims it undoubtedly was, as within its frontiers there was no fully recognized nation or nationality other than the Germans, and the Germans living within these frontiers derived a strong national consciousness from their encompassment within a firmly cemented federal state. In course of time, this led to an unthinking mode of expression, in which the old German nation was split up into "Germans" and "Austrians". To whatever extent German national awareness remained alive or was rearoused in Austria, such a distinction was always dubious. Potentially, an Irredenta of Austrian Germans was developed with respect to the German Empire.

If, therefore, the new German Empire had remained an incomplete national state, in so far as a large part of the nation was not incorporated into it, but could possibly belong to it one day, if there were a change in European conditions, the Empire did on the other hand exceed the boundaries of its own nation in three places. From this situation arose burdensome and dangerous problems of nationality and frontiers, not only in the case of Alsace-Lorraine but also in the Danish and Polish questions.

The Danish minority in northern Schleswig was small and, from the longer view, did not carry much weight in the Reichstag with their one or two representatives. But the Danish question was of importance in principle, because here consideration for an old country-unit had prevented the obvious and, for Bismarck, not fundamentally outrageous solution of dividing Schleswig into a smaller Danish and a larger German area. Instead of this, considerations of power after the wars of 1864 and 1866 led to the incorporation of all of Schleswig into the Empire, without regard for the Danes in the north. Meanwhile the Danes, too, did not desire a division according to language and national allegiance, but had designs on the whole historical duchy of Schleswig, although this was predominantly German. They based their case on the old affiliation to the Danish crown and pinned their hopes on the future. Thus this border question was a burden to the Germans' relations with their northern neighbour for a long time, and Schleswig, like Alsace-Lorraine, was one of the sore points of the young Empire in relation to those European powers who could only achieve their aims through an eventual German defeat.

Of far greater importance was the question of the Poles in the eastern provinces of Prussia. After the Empire had been established as a national state, the traditional possibility faded that there could be Prussians who spoke Polish, Kashubian or Masurian yet did not feel themselves to be Polish or that their only connection with the German nation was through belonging for the time to the Prussian state. The foundation of the Empire as a national state hastened a tendency, that was already under way, for those linguistic and ethnic groups who had not yet decided for modern nationhood to move towards dissolution. In other words, this meant that the innumerable people in the east who until then had not been established as either German or Polish nationals more and more had the decision forced on them from outside whether to opt for the German or the Polish nation.

Immediately after the foundation of the Empire, the struggle between Germans and Poles intensified, firstly over language and schooling and, from 1886 onwards, more strongly than before over occupation of land. The Germanization measures of the Prussian state, culminating after 1886 in the prohibition of the Polish language in schools and the purchase of Polish estates for the purpose of German settlement, were successfully countered by Polish cultural and economic organizations, especially the rural associations, so that there was no question of a decline of the Polish language, ownership of land or national consciousness between 1871 and 1914. The national struggle over land and language, together with the spread of education and prosperity to all classes of society, increased the number of those who consciously identified themselves with one of the two great nations, the Germans, with their state, or the Poles, the nation without a state. In this process, which may be seen as national modernization or as a move towards national democratization, both Germans and Poles made gains. The evangelical Masurians, although for the time being they still used their mother tongue, went over to the German nation in a body. However, amongst great numbers of Kashubian or Polish people in West Prussia and in Upper Silesia there were, for a long time, those of so-called "wavering nationhood": For these people the way from

Prussian to German stood open. But language and adherence to the Catholic Church often stood in the way, and Polish national propaganda, the power-centre of which lay in the province of Posnania, was gradually becoming successful, and at a clearly faster rate after the turn of the century. This was particularly evident in the Reichstag election results for Upper Silesia after 1903. This country, whose population in the middle of the nineteenth century had belonged to neither the German nor the Polish nation, but, regardless of their Polish ("water-Polish") vernacular, had been defined only through the Catholic Church and the Prussian (not German!) state, now began at an increasing pace to split into a Polish and a German half. However, the boundary between the two was not clearly marked, as many had not yet reached the state of national awareness and could react differently to national demands from one side or the other. How far this development had gone in the Empire was shown by the results of the plebiscite in Upper Silesia in 1921, when, in a turn-out of 98%, around 60% voted for Germany and 40% for Poland.

In contrast to the northern part of North Schleswig and also to Alsace-Lorraine, which predominantly inclined towards their neighbouring national state, i.e. towards Denmark and France respectively, there was for the Poles in the Prussian eastern provinces no existing state towards which they could strive. Their national state of the future could only be established in defiance of the three powers who had partitioned Poland amongst themselves after 1793–5, and finally after 1815. Therefore Russia, Austria and Prussia (since 1871 the German Empire) had a common interest in the suppression of the Poles or, if they were to fall out amongst themselves, could play off the Poles against each other. From this basic fact followed the changing history of the Polish nation until the First World War. Whatever the result of this history, especially of the Polish-German national struggle, so much was clear, that Poland could not be resurrected as a national state without losses to the Prussian-German eastern frontier. For, judged on the national principle, this frontier was unjust. But if a situation arose in which Germany should be compelled to make sacrifices of territory for a new Polish state, there was an obvious danger that an injustice in favour of the Germans would become one in favour of the Poles. A clear and impeccably fair borderline between the nations could not be achieved, especially at a time when national passions were being increasingly stirred up by irritant and counter-irritant. Two old and great nations of Europe drifted in a hopeless national struggle towards their mutual destinies.

Thus the frontiers of the German Empire, when seen with due regard for Austria, Alsace-Lorraine, Schleswig and the Polish question, were much more uncertain than most Germans at the time of the Empire were aware. Here was material for future serious conflict, which, however, would only become dangerous in conjunction with external complications. Within the frontiers of the Reich, however, the German nation grew remarkably quickly and strongly into a political unity. What consideration Bismarck had had to give to the German states and their princes in the first years of the establishment of the Empire, even after Austria had withdrawn! The older Bismarck spoke of this in the chapter of his memoirs entitled "Dynasties and Families". "I have never been in any doubt that the key to German politics lay in the princes and dynasties, and not in discussion in parliament and press, or on the barricades". And the emotion of those years around 1870, when he had formed the federation of the new Empire *with* the Princes *in spite of* the diversity of German states, may still be traced when, in the same chapter, written twenty years later, he believed it necessary to underline the point. "If we made the supposition that all the German dynasties were suddenly swept aside, it would not be likely that German national feeling would hold all Germans in legal union amidst the frictions of European politics, not even in the form of federated Hansa towns and imperial villages. The Germans would fall a prey to closer-knit nations if they lost the ties which lie in the shared social assumptions of the princes". It may well be asked whether this judgement was still valid for 1890, when the words were written. Certainly, by the beginning of the world war, Bismarck's judgement had become outdated. The left-wing liberal constitutionalist Hugo Preuss clearly established this when referring these words of Bismarck to the situation in 1915, and in the catastrophe of 1918 it proved that dynasties disappeared within days, but the national unity of the Germans successfully resisted all stresses. That is to say, within the short space of half a century, from the foundation of the Empire to the First World War, the German nation had undergone a complete political change. If, until the sixties, the princely house and its state had loomed larger in the eyes of most Germans as *the* reality before a Germany that politically was barely perceptible, after 1871 it was the Empire as a national state that became tangible reality alongside the princely houses and countries, which were still strongly in evidence. From 1871 on, the scales gradually tipped more and more in favour of the common nation. By the time of William II, the Prussian king had in the eyes of most Germans been pushed into the background by the German emperor, and when the population put out the flags after military victories in the world war, the Prussian black and white was insignificant beside the black, white and red colours of the Empire. By 1914 the Germans of the Empire had become a firmly cohesive nation-state. Their national awareness was bound up in this Empire.

It is profitable to look at the settling of the Germans of the Empire within their national state from the viewpoint of the history of the political parties. At the time of the establishment of the Empire, apart from the weak Free Conservatives ("Imperial Party") based mainly in Silesia and the Rhineland, only the National Liberals were a party of the young national state. All others regarded the new Empire with considerable reserve, even rejected it. The Conservatives stood aside with old Prussian "particularism"; the Progress Party maintained its hostility to Bismarck on principle; the South German democrats (People's Party) were greater Germany minded; the Centre was markedly federalist and greater German in outlook, and was engaged in the bitterly fought *Kulturkampf* with Bismarck and his allies, the National Liberals; finally Bebel, the only social democratic deputy in the Reichstag of 1871, was, like Liebknecht, greater Germany minded, had not voted for the granting of war credits in the North German Reichstag of 1870 and had protested against the incorporation of Alsace-Lorraine into the Empire. It was not without reason that Bismarck, when faced by these attitudes amongst the parties, spoke of "enemies of the Empire". But enemies of the Empire became its friends. The Prussian conservatives reconstituted themselves in 1876 as the "German Conservative Party"; in southern Germany the "People's Party" suffered almost complete defeat in the elections of 1871. Of the 88 South German deputies in the first German Reichstag of 1871, three quarters were already in favour of the Empire and thus no longer anti-Prussian liberals, whilst, apart from two greater-Germany-minded democrats, the remaining quarter belonged to the Centre. This party, however, spread ever more strongly throughout the Empire after the cessation of the *Kulturkampf* in the eighties, and thus increasingly became one of the mainstays of the little German national state, in spite of the unforgotten past, in which they had supported the Austrian solution to the German question. Even the left-wing liberals did not in the end adhere rigidly to their rejection on principle. Their greatest representative in the Wilhelmine period, Friedrich Naumann, turned towards the Emperor, and thus towards the Empire, although in the hope of combining both with democracy. Even social democracy came to terms with the Empire, not, it is true, with its political and social constitution, but only with the German national state as such; the nation was accepted, not as a "class state" but in the coming "people's state". However, in the eyes of the middle classes, the Social Democrats were largely regarded, in the words of William II, as "men without a country", because they belonged to the Internationale and had a Marxist programme. This lack of country, however, only applied to the leadership, and even then not unconditionally. It can have been no surprise to students of social democracy when the latter came out in favour of a national "defensive war" in August 1914.

Thus the point is indicated up to which the Empire was internally strong and beyond which it was fragile. It was strong in respect of the state of unity of the nation. The obstacles to this process had become fewer in the course of the decades. But the Empire was brittle in respect of its constitution. Thus, it was less the unity than the political form of the nation that was called into question. We have seen that the imperial constitution which had come into being in 1867–71 had been not only unattainable in any other way but was also appropriate for its time. But, from the eighties onwards, this was decreasingly the case. Bismarck was continually at loggerheads with the Reichstag and toyed with the idea of reducing its influence, or even abolishing it, by an imposed constitutional reform, as "it was impossible to govern with parliamentarism". It was indeed difficult, given the diversity of the German parties, separated by ideologies and political interests.

Basically, throughout the period of the Empire, the vital question, which was never officially asked, but which unofficially became all the more urgent, remained unresolved: whether to restore a system of monarchical authority, completely independent of the parties, possibly with professional representation, or, conversely, to extend the imperial constitution to the Reichstag, i.e. by introducing parliamentary government on English lines. In the circumstances of the time, both seemed incapable of implementation and would, in fact, have led to such great problems that, in retrospect, the avoidance of painful decisions of this kind can be well understood. The first decision, in accordance with Bismarck's deliberations in the eighties, would have required a *coup d'état* and led to constitutional conflict; authority and nation would have been sharply divided. The decision for a full parliamentary system, on the other hand, would have aroused the resistance of the states and would therefore have been just as impossible to implement as the anti-parliamentary option. If, however, the obstacles thrown up by the federative basis of the Empire could have been overcome and the imperial constitution adapted to a parliamentary system, the way would have been open for all the internal dangers that arise from a parliamentary system with many uncompromising parties, such as did in fact arise in Germany after 1919. Nevertheless, such a course of constitutional reform of the Reichstag would have been in accordance with the development of a more unified national democracy, which was already in process. While it was deliberately avoided, the combination of "democracy and empire" demanded by Friedrich Naumann in 1900 remained unachieved.

A reform in this direction, not unconnected with the continuation of social legislation, was desired by an ever-growing proportion of the nation during the reign of William II. This may be seen in the change in political opinion amongst the imperial population between 1871 and 1912, the year of the last Reichstag elections before the war. It is pre-eminently marked by two events: the sharp decline in the number of non-voters and the corresponding increase in the number of Social Democrats. In other words, in the course of the decades, the nation had become politicized, including the lower class, who at the time of the establishment of the Empire had still been making little use of their universal and equal suffrage. This politicization, however, was moving in the direction of the "people's state", away from the "authoritarian state", as it was expressed in the political catchwords of the period. In summary, the following picture emerges of the variation in political opinion within the main parties, which were occasionally joined by splinter groups, between establishment of the Empire and world war.

The decline in the number of non-voters was almost exactly

Votes in the Reichstag elections in %

	Conserv-atives	National Liberals	Left-wing Liberals	Centre	Region-alists	Social Democrats	Non-voters
1871	11	18	5	9	6	2	48
1890	14	12	13	13	5	14	29
1912	13	12	10	14	5	29	16

balanced by the rise of the Social Democrats and the Centre, which had shot up to 16% in the elections of 1874 as a result of the *Kulturkampf* and had thereafter held level between 13% and 16%. The conservative electors had gained little in strength compared with the time of the establishment of the Empire, while, within liberalism, the predominance of the National Liberals had finally been lost after 1884. The seats in the Reichstag did not fully correspond to the numbers of voters because of the majority vote system and the fact that constituencies had become increasingly unequal in the number of the electorate. For our purpose, it is therefore important to give the distribution of strength in the Reichstag of 1912, because this became the Reichstag of the world war.

Distribution of seats in the 1912 Reichstag in %

Conserv-atives	National Liberals	Left-wing Liberals	Centre	Region-alists	Social Democrats	No party
18	12	11	22	9	28	2

When the problem became acute, only the conservatives amongst these groups were unequivocally opposed to constitutional reform in favour of parliamentarism. Social Democrats and Left-wing Liberals were, in accordance with their programmes, unequivocally for, while the Centre and the National Liberals were equally capable of an about turn, as was seen in 1917. This, then, was how political opinion was constituted in the German nation-state before the outbreak of the First World War. If, in 1871, there had been "hostility to the Empire", in the sense of strong reservations about the little German national state, amongst all the parties except the National Liberals and Free Conservatives, who, however, together made up a majority in the Reichstag, there was scarcely talk of this in 1912; instead, it was a question of hostility to the constitution, with a clearly democratic tendency, in at least half of the Reichstag, while more liberal, Christian, or social democratic reasons were given for this hostility. In 1917 a democratic majority came about in the Reichstag, when Social Democrats, Centre and Progress Party found they shared 61% of the seats and were joined for part of the time by the National Liberals, so that in conjunction with the latter there was even almost a three-quarters majority in favour of representative parliamentary democracy. This majority in the Reichstag reflected a strong feeling amongst the people which was directed against the conservative adherence of William II and his advisers to the current constitution, and against the "feudal" or "militaristic" manifestations of Wilhelmine life-style. This style, as it was practised at court, in officers' messes and in students' associations, setting the tone for a large part of the governing and educated classes, seemed largely anachronistic and provocative. It ran counter to the prevailing political mood of the German people. Their pressure for democracy was an indication of the transformation of the Germans into a people belonging to a modern industrial society. The wage-earners and the "middle class" of tradesmen, officials and employees together made up the great majority of the people. Whereas in 1882 42.5% of those in employment had been engaged in agriculture, against 45.5% in industry, trade and commerce, by 1907 the figures were already 28.6% against 56.2%, and no end to this social transformation seemed to be in sight.

There were, however, considerable obstacles to the great movement for the implementation of constitutional and social democracy. The German Conservatives were still, as had once been the Prussian Conservatives, whose membership they barely exceeded, a "small but powerful party". To them belonged, particularly in Prussia, the leaders of the administration, the military and the Evangelical Church, if not always as members, at least in spirit. Their economic base was the large estates in the east, which, if no longer entirely profitable, were frequently materially improved by marriage alliances with wealthy families from industry, trade or finance. The influence of this leading class was notable; it had a considerable aura, it embodied good, Prussian traditions, which had made many of these families into models of propriety and professional conduct, however much the temptations of social climbing and of the Wilhelmine style had everywhere eroded the old substance. To see this class of "Junkers", together with its middle-class adherents, only through the caricatures of its contemporary opponents or with retrospective superiority is an offence against historical understanding. These men could certainly stand comparison with many other "élites" in history. But they found themselves in an inescapable impasse; for they had been born, or had grown, into their social position and their conservative mentality, and believed themselves bound to oppose the democratic tide of the growing industrial masses because they equated interest in maintaining their position with interest in the preservation of state and society. They therefore had barely any appreciation of the necessity for a constitutional compromise, upon which all other parties (except the extreme left) were agreed, without the Conservatives, in 1917. Thus they were drawn into isolation without any long-term prospects and in 1918, together with the war, they lost their state and their monarchy.

A broad, middle-class nationalist movement which, unlike the Conservatives, who were largely confined to the east, was distributed throughout the Empire, must be judged differently from the backward-looking conservatism of the "Junkers". Its adherents either voted national liberal or gave preference to smaller, right-wing nationalist party-groupings. These right-wing middle classes, on the basis of a strange combination of liberal and conservative philosophy, developed a political mentality which was characterized by the optimism of the rising line, a strong feeling of German importance in the world, the pushing aside of questions of internal reform and a horror of social democracy, for the purpose of fighting which they founded their own national league (*Reichsbund*). Such feelings were not unknown among great numbers of voters of the Centre and even of the left-wing liberal parties, and many observers at that time were forced to the conclusion that the consolidation of the nation was endangered, or even thwarted, by its division into two hostile groups. In "class-placement" and *Weltanschauung* the "nationalist bourgeoisie" and "proletarian socialism" were in direct opposition. There were, it is true, "bourgeois turncoats" in the social democratic, and "nationalist" workers in the "bourgeois", parties. But, apart from the numerous Catholic workers in the party of the centre, these were only exceptions in the general division, by class, mentality and ideology, which was regarded as inevitable and was even exaggerated by agitation on both sides.

In "bourgeois" terms, the division of the people had been driven so far that only they themselves, and not the social democratic workers, could be termed "national". Old social valuations of the nineteenth century played a part in this; by these, the nation, not only in Germany, had been defined by the middle class. But above all it was taken for granted that the Social Democrats were nationally unreliable, or even rejected the nation, as they subscribed to international "working-class solidarity". How greatly the Germans had changed since 1848! Then, not only liberals, but democrats and socialists, had been nationalist, in contrast to the conservatives. Now the national interest was only to be found on the right or, socially, in the "bourgeoisie", and not amongst the Social Democrats. Certainly, in the counter-thrust of political debate, answers enough were given which seemed to confirm this view. For the Social Democrats sharply rejected the specifically middle-class national awareness and national pathos of the Wilhelmine period, not, however, the idea of a nation amongst generally social democratic nations. The rift between middle class and proletariat, nationalists and socialists, had fateful consequences beyond the period of William II. The later legend of the "stab in the back" would not have been possible without this ingrained prejudice, and, not least, Hitler took considerable advantage of this division in the nation.

All these changes and hardening of attitudes had been taking place from about 1895 in conditions of strong economic growth and German participation in the world politics of the imperialist powers. This became clear to the broader German public in the mid-nineties. Friedrich Naumann described the new situation in a series of new reflections; he spoke of future "great acts in world history" and gave the rise of Germany in his time the reassurance of an "optimism on principle" in the conviction that "a nation in the middle of her history" could never "voluntarily blow the whistle to stop". If Bismarck had spoken of his establishment of the Empire as "a final act", Max Weber said in his inaugural speech at Freiburg in 1895: "We must realise that the unification of Germany was a youthful *coup*, carried out by the nation against its past history, and which, on account of its high cost, it would have been better not to undertake if it were the final act and not the starting-point for a policy of German world power."

Further quotations of this kind may be found in abundance. After 1945 the presumptuous arrogance of German utterances in the two decades before the war, often in contributions of distinction, and not infrequently by intelligent publicists and professors, was often singled out. There is no doubt that the period is filled with similar evidence of that exuberance of power which deluded many Germans into dangerously false assessments of their position in the world. It is understandable that this was first recognized, with a sense of shock, and for the greater part discovered historically, only after 1945. But shock must not be allowed to cloud understanding.

The fact that the German Empire around 1900 was developing to the status of a leading economic world power behind, or alongside, the United States and Great Britain had nothing to do with the will to political power. It followed from the intelligence, the enterprise and the, at that time, high working morale of the Germans, based on favourable foundations for heavy industry, especially the plentiful supply of coal. In the age of imperialism, however, when "economic potential" was necessarily an indicator of political and military power, or was converted into this power, this unexpectedly rapid upturn in the economy of the young German state could not but have political consequences. The task naturally facing German policy was to secure recognition of the position gained by Germany in world politics from the nineties onwards, and to make this position decisive for her actions. It was, therefore, less by a conscious decision than as a reaction to the changed world situation that "global politics" (*Weltpolitik*) had to be carried on in Berlin, despite the limitation imposed by Bismarck. There was no way past. The only question was how this was to happen and where the line was to be drawn, which was the important issue for Bismarck, who was always concerned for the preservation of the Empire. Germany's potential was not in any way aided by her position. It was a disadvantage that Germany had entered competition with the world powers later than the Atlantic states of Europe, but it was of greater importance that even larger overseas territories than the Empire possessed would not have neutralized the disadvantage of her position in the middle of the continent. Whereas all the other European powers, and the United States, had been able to spread out over wide areas of land or sea outside Europe, this had not been possible for Germany, who had supplied foreign states with millions of her people in the eighteenth and nineteenth centuries. The Empire remained shut in and, most significantly, could be blockaded from the sea. The more the German industrial state became dependent upon overseas trade, the greater significance this situation acquired. The changed world situation of the German Empire was fundamentally even more dangerous than had been her central position on the European continent. Yet German foreign policy, particularly in the decade of Chancellor von Bülow (1900 to 1909), was largely free of that great concern for the future which had preoccupied Bismarck. There would, however, have been serious cause for concern. For the alliance of flanking powers against the central powers in Europe grew ever tighter, and in fact, from 1904 on, "encirclement" did take place through British rapprochement with France, and from 1907 on, in spite of strong and continuing obstacles, with Russia. A great war of "encirclement", i.e. isolation by land and sea, held no prospect of success for the German Empire, unless, in accordance with the Schlieffen plan, a quick, decisive and total victory could be gained in the western theatre of war.

When we survey the policy of the empire and "public opinion" as a whole before 1914, e.g. in the large organizations of the "national middle classes", the Navy League and the Pan-German Union, we are left with the impression that neither the official leadership of the Empire nor the middle classes of the nation had solved the problem resulting on the one hand from the tension between global politics and economic world power and, on the other, the dangerous "encircled" position of the Empire on the continent if events should move to war. The German nation entered the war with the rift still open between "middle-class nationalist" and "proletarian social-ist", and subject to tension between the ideas of an "endangered central Europe" and her "expansion into global politics".

VII CENTRAL EUROPE – VERSAILLES WEIMAR (1914–32)

In the First World War it was a question for Germany of "world power or downfall", as General Friedrich von Bernhardi had prophetically written in his much-read book *Germany and the Next War* (1912). Today that may sound exaggerated and inaccurate, but this statement tells the modern reader what really was at stake at that time. It is true that the Germans entered a "defensive war" in 1914 with simple faith, and this mood enabled even the Social Democrats to support the nation's war; but, nevertheless, from the first weeks of the war onwards, plans for expansion were drawn up which depended upon conquest and were to be implemented in the peace treaty. These aims were thought of as insurance by the German "world power" against future threats from the few other remaining world powers. This was equally the case with the "defensive wars" of Germany's opponents. Their war aims were, likewise, to preserve their world power, but that meant the neutralization of Germany as a political competitor. These aims were mutually exclusive. A compromise peace was impossible, except as a consequence of the exhaustion of both sides. Thus, once the war had broken out, Germany's situation was accurately described by Bernhardi's alternatives of "world power or downfall".

Certainly, from the outset, "downfall' seemed far more likely for the Empire at war than "world power". Let us leave aside the question whether the strategic principles of the Schlieffen plan, the rapid military annihilation, and therefore neutralization, of France could actually have been achieved. However that may be, everything was basically geared to this unlikely event. If the coup had succeeded, it is highly doubtful whether Great Britain could have prevented almost complete German hegemony on the continent. If the plan failed, however, as was probable, and did in fact happen in the battle of the Marne, then at best there could only be an exhausted peace instead of the probable "downfall', and both sides would have had to forego their war aims. This possibility, however, existed only as long as the war was essentially purely European. If it genuinely became a "world war" through the entry of the United States, then the defeat of Germany, and thus the implementation of Allied war aims against Germany, became inevitable. This was the course actually taken by the war. It therefore led to catastrophe for German world power.

At first, however, events seemed to be taking a different course. After 1914–5 the forces of the Empire and Austria-Hungary occupied large areas in the west (Belgium, northern France) and in the east (Poland, Lithuania, Courland, Serbia); together with Turkish and Bulgarian forces, they conquered Rumania in autumn 1916, Venetia, Riga and Ösel in autumn 1917; in spring 1918 they occupied large areas of White Ruthenia and the Ukraine as well as Esthonia and southern Finland. In March 1918 Russia and, in May 1918, Rumania were compelled to sue for peace, and in August 1918 the peace treaty with Russia was signed. As a result of these treaties all the non-Russian western areas of Russia, i.e. Finland, Esthonia, Livonia, Courland, Lithuania and Poland, together with the Ukraine, were removed from Russian sovereignty. It was anticipated that all these countries would form independent constitutional monarchies, although no exact details had been entered into.

If these peace terms seem just, because peoples and nations had been freed from bonds against which they had fought, secretly or openly, for decades, these "liberations" were nevertheless questionable. Certainly it was by no means the clear will of the Ukrainian people to be separated from Russia. It was even more certain that the Poles were embittered because they had to purchase their desired separation from Russia by an unacceptable diminution of their territory and a grievous restriction of their future sovereignty. Even in the Baltic provinces, decisions were expected which were unsatisfactory to the small, aspiring peoples, the Latvians and the Esthonians. In other words, all the conditions of the Treaty of Brest-Litovsk had the purpose of creating the preconditions for a later "central European" blanket settlement, which would come into effect after the victorious end of the war. In practice, the peoples of the Russo-German border area were to transfer from Russian to German or German-Austro-Hungarian control, whilst they themselves, at least in their upper and educated classes, desired to become "sovereign" national states. The consequence was that in all the nations concerned, most of all among the Poles and least of all among the Finns, who had experienced German friendship and had nothing to fear from them, the Treaty of Brest-Litovsk lives on in the national memory as an imposed "imperialistic" peace, even though it first created the conditions for the later foundation of national states.

The leadership of the German Empire, and the German people, although they were still under the influence of their great military successes and were hoping for a favourable outcome to the war, were faced between 1915 and 1918 with the question of "Central Europe". Even if this seems unreal *post festum*, and is retrospectively branded as reprehensible by political moralists, in the situation of the First World War "Central Europe" was a genuine possibility which, if not actually striven for, must at least be considered. Unless German policy was consistently based on a defensive war without annexations, with the aim of preservation of the status quo, then it must of necessity develop the conception of a peace settlement which would be in accordance with German interests in the age of imperialism and could also be justified to the outside world. When it came to the effective and credible fixing of such a peace settlement, Germany was inferior to her opponents. As German policy had no political ideology which even appeared to contain a principle for universal improvement and could be used for a world-wide appeal to the peoples of the earth, German propaganda had to take a back seat during the war. From conquered Russia, the peace decree of the Bolshevist revolutionary government of November 1917 rang out throughout the world: the offer of a "just and democratic peace, longed for by the overwhelming majority of the working classes of all warring nations, exhausted, tortured and tormented by the war", of a peace without annexations and in accordance with the right of nations to self-determination. Behind this appeal was the conviction of Lenin and his collaborators of a future great success for the "world revolution". Shortly after, the American President Wilson proclaimed in his speech of 8 January 1918 to Congress, in which he announced his Fourteen Points for peace, that the age of war and of secret diplomacy was at an end, and that the era of world peace was beginning. "What we demand in this war, therefore, is nothing peculiar to ourselves. It is that the world be made fit and safe to live in". The general principle was to be that every nation could determine its own future, and should be protected by binding laws, and that use of force and "self-seeking aggression" must never again be possible in future. From this developed Wilson's idea of a League of Nations, by means of which general peace and justice were to be assured for all in the future. These conceptions, Lenin's world revolution and Wilson's league for world peace, were, of course, mutually exclusive and entered into competition throughout the world, but at first, in practice, they were both directed at Germany in particular, in the hope of subjecting the German nation to their ideal. Thus, two schemes of moral redemption were born which were more than mere theoretical plans for world peace of the kind that had often been seen before; for behind both programmes stood a great power, even if one of them had, for the time, been militarily defeated. Both programmes filtered into Germany and weakened the home front of the heavily burdened empire.

The Germans lacked a missionary interpretation of the war with which to counter the American or the Russian message successfully. Not that a moral justification of the war was unavailable. But this was only of help to the Germans themselves and had hardly any influence on other peoples. It was, first and foremost, the feeling of having been systematically "encircled" by enemies and driven into war, because France wanted to have her "satisfaction" and because England especially had been jealous of the rise of the Germans, even though English and Germans were closely related peoples whose interests did not need to conflict. The feeling that it was England who had allied herself with the enemies of Germany and thus exposed the Empire to mortal danger was very bitter. Thus animosity to *perfide Albion* greatly exceeded hatred of the French "traditional enemy", especially at the start of the war. "God punish England" was the slogan of the Germans who thought right was on their side. Allied with the feeling that they must defend themselves against the destructive will of their enemies was pride in their own achievement and superiority in face of their opponents' predominance in men and material. "Many foes, much honour". The need to provide security against enemy expansionism even in the period after the war provided the moral justification for expansionist war aims, not only in the west, but especially in the east against the "Russian menace" of the future. Thus the Germans had in mind, however different the individual solutions proposed might be, a "Central Europe" stretching far to the east under the leadership of the two central powers united in a strong alliance, not an "imperialist" repression of other peoples, but rather a safety measure on a European level, to prevent future Russian aggression.

The left-wing liberal politician, Friedrich Naumann, expressed the widely felt conviction that modern, technical and economic development into a "large-scale political concern" was a matter of urgency and that the decisive historical question of the world war was whether Europe, though that meant first and foremost a Central Europe led by Germany after the defeat of the French, would be able to continue to exist as such a "large-scale concern" between, on the one hand, the maritime powers of the United States and Great Britain, which would continue in the future to be geostrategic-ally favoured, and, on the other hand, the continental land-mass of the Russians. In Naumann's conception, this Central Europe was to grant individual peoples full linguistic and cultural freedom within their own national states. These states were, however, to be stripped of their sovereignty, as they were to have the advantage of the common foreign policy, the common army and the unifying economic policy of the "large-scale concern". This was a federally minded solution which did not dispense with the political logic of the historical moment. Only Naumann's ideal picture did not match the stronger tendencies of the "annexationists", who were influential in the state administration as well as the economy. General Ludendorff was their most powerful spokesman. This became particularly clear in the case of Poland. Although that country was proclaimed a future independent kingdom within the Central European framework on 5 November 1916, far from being assigned old Polish areas in Prussian-German or Austrian possession, like the province of Posnania or West Galicia, she was still further cut up by a strategically based "border-area" between East Prussia and Upper Silesia. In the east, also, Poland was to remain enclosed and permitted no expansion into the Lithuanian-White Ruthenian area. A Poland "laced up" like this after Ludendorff's conception was a contradiction of the idea of a justly federated Central Europe. So idea and reality were not in accord. What was lacking was the kind of political leadership which did more than merely react to the current constraints of the war situation or the pressure of the internal and half-public dispute over war aims. Externally, however, the programme of a Central European Confederation of a diversity of constitutional monarchies under the primacy of the Hohenzollern and the Habsburg Emperors was hardly persuasive. Central Europe as a political idea foundered with the military defeat of 1918.

In a different way, however, it outlived the end of the war. For the eyes of Germans in the empire had been reopened by the events of the war, not least by the experience of many German soldiers on the eastern front, to eastern central Europe, the reality of which was now suddenly no longer concealed by the title "Russian Empire". The many German language islands far to the east were, in a sense, rediscovered. And, in reverse, the mainly peasant people of these language islands were torn from a political order that had seemed eternal, and confronted with German power reaching out to the east, the power of their own nation which they had not previously experienced in a political sense. Thus their lives were exposed to a profound convulsion. More even than in the last decades before the world war, when part of these scattered settlements had been threatened with Russianization, they were now faced with the political problem of being German in a foreign environment. What position were these Germans to expect in a Central Europe led by Germany? What would be their lot if Germany lost the war? Could or should they feel themselves to be members of the German nation in the political sense of the word? How could that be combined with membership of another state? The scattered Germans who were politically reawakened by the world war were placed in this state of tension after 1919 and remained in it until the bitter end in the Second World War.

While the Germans beyond the imperial frontiers were thus becoming increasingly nationally politicized, the German nation within the frontiers was forced more strongly than before into a "popular community" by the trial of strength of the Great War. As in the other great European nations at the beginning of August 1914, a wave of national enthusiasm for the war swept through the whole people, now no longer divided into middle classes and proletariat. Never before and never again was there in Germany such a tumultuous mass affirmation of the "people in arms". In 1939 little could be traced of this youthful, naïve outburst, with its ignorance of modern warfare, of the trusting nation of 1914. Painful experience separated these two dates, and in 1939 many sensed impending disaster. In 1914, however, there was a general readiness to make sacrifices for the good, even "holy" cause of the Fatherland, without there being any conception of the scale of future sacrifice. In this "spirit of 1914" the nation entered the Great War, and essentially, in spite of all the almost unbearable burdens, this spirit lasted until the end of the war. The Emperor's dictum that he knew no more parties, only Germans, was popular, and the political truce (*Burgfriede*) was taken completely seriously by almost everyone from the beginning. But the longer the war lasted beyond the optimistic expectations of its early days, the more urgent became the questioning whether it was not after all in the spirit of the political truce and the popular community to make a start towards democratic reforms even during the war; that is to say, to drop the Prussian three-class system of voting and to introduce parliamentarism into the constitution of the Empire. The leadership of the Empire, however, adhered to the view that the "new course" must wait until after the end of the war, and the Conservatives, now as ever, closed their ranks against any development of the constitution in a democratic direction. Thus the fire smouldered beneath the political truce, the more so as privation grew, hunger increased and victory seemed less in prospect.

In this situation, after long internal preparation, the Social Democratic Party split up in 1917. The independent social democrats decided against war credits, thereby expressly rejecting the national war in favour of the future revolution of international proletarian solidarity, and no longer held to the political truce. The social democratic majority against this split were thus put in a difficult situation. On the one hand, they were now free of those elements who had barred the way to discussions with the democratically minded parties. On the other hand, there was the danger of losing credibility as a *socialist* party in face of mounting need. Nevertheless, their leaders, particularly Ebert and Scheidemann, consciously followed a course of constitutional compromise with the Centre and the Progress Party, with whom they entered the so-called Interparty Alliance of the German Reichstag in July 1917, the time of the peace resolution supported by these three parties. Parliamentarians within this majority of the Reichstag, joined for a time by the National Liberals, were united by the knowledge of a double necessity: internally, they desired to smooth the way to democracy, at that stage still in conjunction with the monarchy; externally, they sought salvation from destruction by urging peace without annexations, i.e. the *status quo*. In doing so, however, they stumbled into the crossfire of the mutually exclusive war programmes of the two hostile sides, which were rigidly adhered to. However desirable democracy and a negotiated peace might be, and however much this combination represented the best imaginable solution, it was nevertheless unrealistic in face of the stiffening of the war fronts and the rising prospect of an Allied victory after the entry into the war of the United States, and especially so since the appearance of the Americans in the western theatre in summer 1918. In Germany, the Emperor and the two chancellors after Bethmann-Hollweg, not least because of pressure from Ludendorff, refused to recognize the inevitable. The "Fatherland Party" was founded to keep the idea of victory alive in the people, for this must never be doubted, to counter the peace resolution of the parliamentary majority. In England and France, however, hope was growing that their war aims were approaching realization. It was taken for granted by the British and French leadership that victory must be exploited for their own reasons of state and in accordance with their set aims, and Wilson's general aims must only enter their calculations to the extent that, generously interpreted, they could be made to coincide with the war aims.

In July 1917, in reaction to the peace resolution in the Reichstag, Max Weber had already turned against this illusion. "Parliamentarism to bring peace! Sheer nonsense, for who is interested? To combine talk of democracy with the hope of peace is a serious mistake." Abroad, this would be seen as weakness. But, internally, people would say, "These concessions have been made under pressure from abroad." This was "a wretched tale". Here Max Weber had touched on the core of the fateful difficulty of transition from war to peace. The ideological moralizing surrounding war and peace led to false hopes and fundamental errors of interpretation of the situation. The wide expectations in Germany of a just and generous "Wilson peace" rested on some such view as this: the war was being fought by the west for the spread of democracy. If Germany altered her constitution accordingly in a democratic direction, and if, in addition, she were led by new, democratic men, then there would be no forced settlement which, for example, ran counter to the democratic right to national self-determination; then it must surely be a settlement which would satisfy all nations, even the conquered, and thus would guarantee lasting world peace in the future. This must be in the general interest. After such a settlement, a democratic Germany, even if she were made to suffer some losses, would not seek revenge or a new extension of her powers at the expense of others. Rather she would accommodate herself honourably and in good faith to a general world of democracies at peace. Germany must become democratic and, as they put it in October 1918, allow the Emperor to abdicate. Then she would be granted a "good" peace. But the obverse of this view ran: if the victorious powers refuse a "Wilson peace", they will have revealed the hypocrisy of their democratic phrases and shown their true colours. The resistance of a wronged people must be roused against such immorality. This must be resistance not only against the enemies in the war, but at the same time, and primarily, a fight against the democratic government and state of their own Empire. Democracy had come with defeat; it was imported by the victors and found unsuitable for the German people, who must prove themselves superior to "western" democracy.

Thus the destiny of the German nation was decided both in the democratic illusion and in the anti-democratic "revelation" of the change of 1918–9. At that moment the nation was not prepared from within, nor did she receive help from without, to adapt realistically to her situation, which had inevitably and irreversibly changed. The task to be undertaken in order to meet the new position was: to resolve internal tension by democratization of state and society, and to recognize the fact that the German Empire was no longer one of the first order of world powers, the "large-scale political concerns". The main burden of German history in the years after 1918 can be summarized in the question to what extent it was possible to understand the new situation and to make it the starting-point for a German policy based on that situation. The following details should be stressed:

In October and November of 1918, the fundamental changes took place in quick succession; "Central Europe" broke up; Austria-Hungary fell apart; the monarchies in Vienna, Berlin and all the other German capitals disappeared without resistance; the socialist revolution broke out; the armistices on the French and Italian fronts did not mean a cease-fire of still effective armies, but rather forced the complete disarming of Imperial German and Austro-Hungarian forces. Internal and external questions, revolution and peace settlement, all were inextricably confused. Although by the Armistice of 11 November the German Empire had ceded its independent rights of negotiation and was delivered helpless into the hands of the victors, the hope of a "Wilson peace" contributed to the strengthening of democratic forces within the Empire. Ebert, and with him the leading social democrats, had neither wanted a revolutionary civil war beforehand nor wanted to make it the means to a socialist seizure of power now when, beginning with the naval mutiny, it had broken out. In conjunction with the High Command of the Army which, in accordance with the armistice conditions, had led its forces in good order back over the Rhine before demobilizing the great majority, the revolution was nipped in the bud and, later too, it was repeatedly put down militarily when it flared up again. Workers' and soldiers' councils were set up within this general outlook. Thus order was maintained, although with difficulty; wages went on being paid, and food supplies were not interrupted, even if it was only a starvation diet. Thanks to these internal achievements, the occupation of Germany by Allied troops was avoided, and the unity of the Empire preserved. Many dangers seemed to have disappeared. It was not without hope for the future that the Germans of the Empire went to the polls in January, and those of German Austria in February. For the first time women too were allowed to vote. In the Empire, there was a three-quarters majority of the three parties of the constitutional compromise of 1917: 38% Social Democrats, 20% Centre and 19% German Democrats. The parties to the right and the left were only weak. In the Viennese constituent national assembly, the two big parties, Social Democrats and Christian Socialists, gained over four-fifths of all the seats in roughly equal shares; the rest went essentially to the German nationalist right.

Hopes for the peace settlement were joined to the expectation that German Austria, whose Provisional National Assembly had already on 12 November 1918 declared "German Austria a democratic republic and component part of the German Empire", could be united with the German Empire within a German national state. The Habsburg empire had quickly dissolved in such a way that either new, independent national states emerged, like Hungary and Czechoslovakia, or the peoples of the old monarchies attached themselves to their national states, like the Poles, the Rumanians, the southern Slav Slovenes, Croatians and Serbs, as also the Italians. For the Germans likewise there seemed to be only one logical conclusion; thus the desire for union was unanimous, not only in Austria, but also in the Empire. The National Assembly in Weimar expressly declared itself in favour. However, it was in accordance with the orderly, proper course of political change in Germany and German Austria that national revolutionary self-help, of the type often and variously applied by other peoples in eastern central Europe, was not invoked. It was expected that the peace settlement would remove the frontier markers in accordance with the principle of self-determination. Thus the chance of rapid union was missed. It was destroyed by French objections. For Clemenceau the population of the German Empire was still too great, even after the cessions of territory in 1919-20; how could a further enlargement of the population by union with the German areas of Austria be tolerated! Thus German Austria, in the guise of the "Republic of Austria" embarked upon a hard new period of her history. Although at the beginning, at a time of national need, there was not a great reaction amongst the people, the union movement remained strong; in Tyrol and Salzburg there were plebiscites, which were virtually unanimous demonstrations in favour of the German national state. But when further plebiscites were discontinued and the urgently necessary scheme for economic aid from the western powers was made conditional upon the strangling of the union movement, people in Austria began to come to terms with necessity and to settle themselves, with continued financial aid from abroad, within their own "independent" state. However, the German Austria question was by no means solved, merely shelved.

A particular problem was presented by the question of the Germans in Bohemia and Moravia, i.e. in the main areas of newly-formed Czechoslovakia, a question which had only been settled by force and against the principle of self-determination. There, too, the Germans had been in favour of union. Amongst the counter-arguments of the Czechs was the old, undeniable thesis of the unity of historical countries, which were not to be torn apart by the boundaries of modern national states. In addition, it was stressed that the Czechs, who were in future to be united with the Slovaks in the new nation-state of the Czecho-Slovaks, not only promised correct guarantees for foreign national minorities but even spoke of the ideal of a "Central European Switzerland". However honestly Masaryk may have meant this, it was an illusion. For the Swiss had grown in the course of centuries, i.e. since the pre-revolutionary era, into a confederation, and in the nineteenth century from this into a modern nation. In Czechoslovakia in 1919, however, nations were thrown together which had long been engaged in national struggles and which had absolutely no will to form a nation-state together. It could not be expected that they would give up their conflicting claims in favour of a new state structure that appeared "artificial" to the minorities. However, in Bohemia and Moravia after 1919, as in Austria, there developed an acceptance of the inevitable status quo. But here too there could be no talk of a solution which could be regarded as lasting or enjoying the confidence of the population; and that must remain the case for as long as eastern central Europe as a whole remained unsettled, in spite of the peace treaties of 1919, 1920 and 1921, with its numerous problems of frontier, nationality and Irredenta.

The crumbling of Austria-Hungary and the reorganization of eastern central Europe into many national states, which were actually nationality states, had created for the German nation not only Irredenta problems, as in "German Austria" and with the "Sudeten Germans", but also the presence of a new "minority" in young national democracies with unsettled political and social constitutions. This was the final step in the development of the German language islands in eastern central Europe, which were discussed earlier. Their ethnic separation, which had frequently come close to being complete isolation, was finally at an end. The national democratization of the former Austria-Hungary and the western areas of the defunct Tsarist empire had serious consequences for the scattered Germans; they were differentiated from the Germans within the main unit and yet were brought nearer to them. From the national democratic principle it followed either that the old national groups were absorbed into the surrounding people, who formed a nation-state in 1918, or that the Germans of a country organized themselves into unions to preserve themselves from this process and appeared in parliamentary parties as a "national group" or a "minority". The way had been prepared for all this a long time before in the Viennese Imperial Diet, which had been elected by universal and equal suffrage for the first time in 1907, and to a lesser extent also within the Tsarist empire. After the end of the First World War, however, it became very clear, and happened of necessity, because all the young states of eastern central Europe received democratic constitutions, although, except in the case of Czechoslovakia, these soon gave way to more or less authoritarian governments.

Many new conflicts of nationality resulted from this situation in the post-war period. The Germans were not the only ones, but were the most affected. In more or less open discussion, the alternatives were: assimilation or national self-assertion; political co-operation (e.g. in coalition governments) with the people of the state, or isolated opposition; recognition of the frontier settlement of 1919 in the hope of a gradual diminution of national feuds, either with the aid of the League of Nations or in a future federated Europe, or to wait for the collapse of the system established by the peace treaties; political adherence to the German nation even as citizens of other national states, or a definite limitation to mere cultural autonomy; sincere loyalty to the state of which they were citizens, or reservations towards the state-system, which was not seen as permanent, and whose policy of assimilation was felt to be restricting or threatening. These questions arose in all eastern central European states. Thus, even if considerably changed, the central European problem of the First World War was still present. The influence of the leaders of the German and non-German ethnic groups was by no means calming; remarkable proposals were made for the pacification of ethnic unrest in central Europe, especially by the European Nationality Congress of 1925.

However the problem might develop, whether as a whole or in its individual manifestations, it was certain that, as a result of the twin events of the Great War and the ensuing peace settlement, the Germans of eastern central Europe, as far as the most remote rural language islands, grew together nationally and politically. This was a necessary consequence of events between 1914 and 1919 as well as of the general national democratization of eastern central Europe. It was inevitably a politically explosive position, especially in a situation of general emotion after the experience of the "World War", in which the nation of the European centre had first gained great victories and then suffered an even greater defeat. The more highly then must we estimate the way in which the leaders of the organized ethnic groups recognized their responsibility and fulfilled their difficult task, of creating a "national identity" which was without a national state yet loyal to the foreign national state which, for them, was "home".

The Germans of the Empire now became more strongly aware of the position of the German people in the scattered eastern settlements than they had been before the war. The "Association for Germans Abroad" ensured a wide dissemination of the idea of a community of German people beyond the frontiers of the Empire, especially amongst young people. On many "journeys", these young people, particularly those belonging to branches of the Youth Movement, discovered the life of German groups abroad. This, incidentally, provided a new justification in Germany for the increasing use of the word "people" in contrast to the "western" concept of "nation". The uniqueness of the German people compared with the western nations was seen in the fact that the latter could only be comprehended by their state frontiers, whereas the "people" was independent of state frontiers, existed outside them and represented not only a cultural and linguistic, but also a political, entity. Such accurate observations, which were based on the facts of a long, unique national history, were often exaggerated in the twenties into popular-national imaginings and ideologies which greatly contributed to the confusion of political opinion in the emotion of the years after 1918. Taken as a whole, the Germans of the Empire were, naturally enough, mainly taken up with the needs of their own state and thus of their nation-state, a situation which often gave rise to tension between politicians of the wider view and those concerned only with the politics of the narrower German state.

If the peace treaties of Versailles, St. Germain and the Trianon had been decisive for the reorganization of central Europe in general, the German Empire, and thus the German nation-state, was affected only by the Treaty of Versailles. As the main event in German history directly after the First World War, its effects were extraordinarily extensive and profound. Certainly its conditions were milder than those imposed upon the Germans in 1945. Nevertheless, the 1919 treaty had a far more inflammatory effect than the provisional regulations of 1945, which were followed by no peace treaty at all. For in 1919 everything was lacking which in 1945 led to the German nation resigning itself to the inevitable: namely, the feeling of guilt after great outrage, the experience of complete impotence without their own state, the knowledge that a condition of at least "cold" war was continuing, in which the victors were entangled and into which they soon drew the Germans after them, and finally the realization that the world had changed, was continuing to change rapidly and could no longer be linked with the period before the war.

The Peace of Versailles was neither a "Wilson peace" nor a "Carthaginian" peace, such as was occasionally discussed in the victors' camp. Its individual conditions were materially hard; when measured by democratic principles, especially that of the right to self-determination, they were unjust; finally, in the paragraphs concerning the question of war-guilt, called "shameful" by the Germans, they were deeply wounding. Also it was no longer a peace in the tradition of European peace treaties since the seventeenth century. For there were no negotiations with the defeated. Hence the Germans spoke of the *Diktat* of Versailles. Among the ranks of the "peacemakers", even in the secret discussions of the "Big Three", Wilson, Lloyd George and Clemenceau, the dubiousness and the brittleness of the peace were fully realized. There were harsh disagreements, which led finally to Wilson's physical and mental collapse. That the German people of all parties rose up against this peace, and that the treaty was eventually signed in Versailles under the pressure of an Allied ultimatum in face of material need, military weakness and the endangering of the unity of the Empire, was like a thorn in the German consciousness in the twenties, and it was continually exploited by agitators. The revision of the Treaty of Versailles became the natural aim of German policy. On the side of the victorious powers this desire for revision was met partly by stiff insistence on the letter, partly by a readiness to compromise. English policy soon inclined to the latter; France, hesitantly and partly resisting, also followed this course from 1924 onwards. There was, however, complete agreement in the west that the injustice of the "Diktat" should not be too strongly emphasized, but rather that the justice of this victory in a "good cause" should be kept alive in historical memories.

After Hitler had made the "*Diktat* of Versailles" the basis of his political campaign, had started his chain of conquests and shameful deeds under the banner of this "good cause", and had thus cast Germany into the abyss, the Germans began to distance themselves from Versailles. Calmer consideration even of this fateful wound of 1919 thus became possible. However, the modern tendency, for well-intentioned reasons of understanding, to play down the Treaty of Versailles, and to dismiss the serious historical question it poses into the psychological area of a "Versailles complex", will not stand up to historical criticism. The fearful harshness of the situation in 1919 cannot be softened, even in historical retrospect. This harshness is not diminished by the knowledge that a German victory would presumably not have been followed by any more generous a peace.

As a result of Versailles, the conditions for the development of political awareness and will in the German nation were considerably changed. At the beginning of 1919 it had seemed as if the situation was open. This had been expressed in the elections for the Weimar National Assembly. But then came the blow from without, by which for the first time the consequences of defeat had been brought home to all Germans in their full seriousness. The imperial government under the social democratic Minister President Scheidemann pronounced "unacceptable" the peace terms announced to the German delegation in Versailles at the beginning of May 1919. Soon after, the government resigned. A new one, without the German Democrats, was formed by Social Democrats and Centrists, and this government took it upon itself to accept the "unacceptable" after all. While the food situation was still bad, the transition from a wartime to a peacetime economy by no means completed and the danger of revolution from the left not yet banished, emotions were aroused over details of the peace treaty: over plebiscites and transfers of territory, over disarmament and reduction of the army, whose soldiers were not to be provided for, over deliveries and the question of reparations, not least over the demanded delivery of the Emperor and of "war criminals", and over the "war-guilt lie". All this together caused not only bitterness and hatred, but also hopelessness for the future and scepticism about the political course which was the only possibility for the nation after the collapse of the Empire: internally, creation of a democratic republic and, externally, a review of policy with the aim of fitting Germany into a new European political system.

There was, indeed, good reason for such scepticism. Of fateful consequence was the way in which a large proportion of Germans who had taken up a neutral stance to the changed German situation at the beginning of 1919 now reacted. Only now were the full consequences of the combination of democracy, defeat and the divisiveness of the new peace settlement apparent. The critics on the right quickly found obvious arguments. Disillusionment worked in their favour. The "wave from the right" flooded the three-quarters majority of the young democracy of January 1919. In the Reichstag elections of June 1920 the two right-wing parties had more than doubled their vote. And as the radical left also had almost quadrupled in strength at the expense of the Social Democrats, the governing three-quarters majority had shrunk to a minority. The "wave from the right" most benefited two parties who opposed the newly introduced, old flag of the Revolution of 1848 with the symbol of the Empire, the black, white and red flag: the German People's Party of Gustav Stresemann, the successor to the national liberals, which, however, soon showed a readiness for compromise and coalition with the democratic centre, and the German National People's Party, the successor to the conservative, Christian-socialist and also partly anti-Semitic parties. These German national parties became the meeting ground in the decade after 1919 of all those who were more uncompromisingly set against democracy than the German People's Party. The Party was never able to become a great conservative party within the existing constitution, that is with the aim of combining conservatism and democracy. In practice, it predominantly followed the model of the departed monarchy and, firmly in the tradition of "middle-class nationalism" and the "Fatherland Party", claimed to represent the "national opposition" rather then the democrats, who were not "national".

In the word "national", therefore, was expressed a hostility in principle to the new form of the state. National opposition meant hostility to the republic, its constitution and its "compliant politicians", who were soft in relation to the victorious powers. To be national meant to be right-wing, against democracy and Versailles. The conservative and "nationally" minded supporters of the Empire were now the "imperialist enemies" of the democratic republic. It was, of course, clear that in the long run such a negative attitude, with its outdated standards, must solidify and decline in influence. As the Weimar Republic grew stronger within and without, and this started clearly in 1924, the "national opposition" lost votes. From 1924 to 1928, for the German Nationalists alone, they fell from around 20% to 14%. If we include the "German People's Party" or the "National Socialist Liberation Movement", then the decline was even more marked: from 26% to 17%. That is to say, as the Republic continued its peaceful development, the wave from the right ebbed again and showed a readiness, after it had adapted to the new environment, to accept the existing constitution and to help to convert what was possible into reality. With the ageing or the death of those who had held responsible posts in the professions at the time of William II and with the advent of younger men to whom imperial tradition meant less, the monarchist past lost its attraction, indeed increasingly stood under the odium of being a model only for "reactionaries". When the wave from the right clearly began to rise again with the beginning of the economic crisis in 1929, it did not, this time, work in favour of the German national monarchists but of those who maintained that genuine "nationalism" was to be found in neither the "democrats" nor the "reactionaries". What was more important was to banish parties altogether beyond the outdated fronts of left and right and to create a true "people's community" of "national socialism". Whoever wanted to be "national" in the true sense must not look back, but forward; he must be revolutionary. "Middle-class nationalism" was no effective answer to the "Marxism" that was undermining the nation.

This appeal of Hitler's had great success. Thus a remarkable change in the consciousness of the German nation had become visible. The tendency to return to the state and society of a conservative monarchy had finally disappeared. There was a general "democratic" feeling in favour of a popular government concerned for the welfare of the masses. However, there remained a widespread mistrust, open or concealed, of the practicability of parliamentary democracy. If conditions becoming critical seemed to confirm this impracticability, then the obvious course was to seek salvation beyond parliamentarism and "reaction", in Hitler. Confidence in the democratic republic, constantly shown from 1920 onwards by only half of the electorate, but in 1928 again by about 60%, was increasingly and finally undermined after 1930. Thus the world economic crisis interrupted the strengthening of the democratic national state, which had been making progress in spite of the weakness of a parliament with a multiplicity of parties. The German nation-state faced the most severe crisis in its modern history.

An upturn in Germany's external position was also unmistakable in the middle years of the Weimar Republic. Belatedly, but not too late, the Empire was accepted into the League of Nations at Geneva in 1926, after the Treaty of Locarno had shown the way and France needed have no further fears for her eastern frontiers after the renunciation of all claims to Alsace-Lorraine. Thus Germany had been fitted into the European post-war system. The League of Nations offered a move towards further policies for frontier revision and minorities. The idea of a more closely federated Europe shifted from mere journalism into the area of serious political consideration. It was true that German policy for frontier revision and French plans for Europe were mutually exclusive. But what hopeful progress could nevertheless be seen in the fact that Briand and Stresemann were "Europeans" and friends, that the two supposedly "traditional enemies" were drawing closer politically, culturally and economically! In spite of the counter-propaganda of the "national opposition" in both countries, an awareness spread that the path to Europe could only lead via Franco-German understanding. Certainly, all this was only a start, but a significant one. Here, too, the political burdens of the great economic crisis had a hampering effect, though this continued to some extent in the National Socialist period.

If, in the west, Germany was part of a consolidated Europe in which there were no more territorial disputes, the Treaty of Locarno having resolved all frontier questions, in the east she extended into the still unsettled zone of eastern central Europe. There the policy of the Empire was not only morally committed to the cause of the German minorities, but the Empire itself was in harsh friction with "blood-soaked frontiers". German-Polish relations in particular, now between two states and nation-states, were hopelessly poisoned by the drawing of the frontiers and the new questions of ethnic groups. Stresemann had withdrawn from an "eastern Locarno", i.e. guaranteed acceptance of the German eastern frontier. The governments of the Empire made no concealment of the fact that they desired the revision of the frontier, which ran largely counter to the right to self-determination, especially for Danzig and Upper Silesia. The public on both sides was inflamed. Over half a million Germans of the lost eastern territories had left, partly voluntarily, partly under Polish pressure. Scholarship and journalism on both sides were busily engaged in historically undermining German or Polish claims. There were virtually no serious political attempts to break out of the fateful circle of German-Polish opposition.

If we review Germany's external situation in the twenties as a whole, the most striking feature is her confined position within the continent, in contrast to the expansiveness of her position in the world of 1914. Germany was no longer "encircled" by three world powers, only by France, Poland and Czechoslovakia, which were in military alliance and so superior to Germany, the former world power, that an action against one of the three states had no prospect of success and was militarily conceivable only in terms of defensive delaying tactics. The German nation as a whole, within and without the imperial frontiers, was so diversely and pettily bound up in restrictive controversies that she remained insufficiently aware of her position in the world beyond Europe. Hardly had this begun to change in the middle years, after the short upturn in the economy, than the Germans were once more thrown back into internal disorder and central European confinement by the great crisis. Thus, for example, there were not even effective links with the politics and culture of the United States of America, which could obviously have followed from close economic contact.

Historical judgement of the history of the German nation at the time of the Weimar Republic is still very difficult up to the present day because we think mainly in terms of "fourteen years", and these fourteen years can easily be seen too much in isolation. If we call to mind the legacy of the Empire and the burden of early 1918–9, and if we highlight the crisis-ridden years of 1919 to 1923 and 1929–32, in which there was no room for manoeuvre, only great masses of people, suffering intensely, cramped up in conditions of political fever, then only four or five years are left in the middle in which the beginnings of a calmer, more realistic, more appropriate development of the nation were visible. But they were only a beginning. Even in those years, the German nation as a whole had not known how to establish itself with sure instinct in a changed world. The statesmen of the democratic parties, especially of social democracy, who were the important ones at the start, were hardly, for all their honesty and efficiency, political figures of outstanding calibre. On the whole, democracy remained internally too strongly on the political defensive, and thus from 1930 to 1932, when it was important to lead and to fight decisively, it was not ready to meet the critical situation. Thus Hitler was able, in the years of major crisis, to direct the counter-current which had been there from the beginning and had not ebbed in the middle years. It was the expression of a nation confused, wounded and disappointed by a rapid ascent, the experience of war and a rapid fall. This counter-current consisted of a feeling of contempt for representative parliamentary democracy, and the conviction that the Germans as a people of strength, order and efficiency must force their way up again against all resistance from within and without. To some extent this reflected a healthy will to survive and an understandable reaction to the humiliation of the post-war years; but it also contained the risk of greatly underestimating the moral and material strength of other nations, like the still too little known Americans, and of failing to achieve a sufficiently accurate sense of the proportions of the post-war world.

VIII NATIONAL SOCIALISM AND
GERMAN NATION

We have seen that National Socialism did not become a mass movement until 1930, that is to say, until the great economic crisis. Thus the question which concerns us, that of the connection between National Socialism and the German nation, did not begin to acquire historical significance until that time.

Nevertheless, the antecedents of the National Socialist era must not be entirely ignored. Much that is often unsatisfactory, or even false, has been written on this topic. (William L. Shirer's widely read book on the rise and fall of the Third Reich has re-disseminated the most extreme misinterpretation of this history, one also propagated before Shirer. According to this view, Hitler's National Socialism, in word and action, was nothing less than the logical outcome of the German national character and the errors of German history, as had already become terribly clear in the cases of, for example, Luther, Frederick the Great and Bismarck. With an absurd assertion of this nature, not only is German history fundamentally misinterpreted and the attempt at historical understanding rejected in advance, but the implications of National Socialism on a supranational level, and as a phenomenon of the period, in its combination of mass movement and totalitarian power-structure, are overlooked.)

Our survey of German history since the Napoleonic era has already indicated in many places, although the point has not been particularly stressed, factors contributing to the preconditions for National Socialism, some remote in time and others directly preceding it. In the nineteenth century elements were already recognizable in the early national movement which later emerged, grossly distorted, within National Socialism. However, the course of German history itself is more important than the search for earlier, spiritual precursors. It was of fateful, long-term significance that the German national movement did not develop freely, but was dammed up for a long time, released for a moment – 1848 – immediately held back again and then developed from the sixties onwards in a new atmosphere of *Realpolitik*, without, however, ever reaching complete fulfilment. For Bismarck's Empire had remained incomplete in two respects: externally by the exclusion of 9.5 million Germans (1910) in Austria, and internally by the refusal of a move to a fully democratic parliamentary constitution. Both questions had once more appeared on the political agenda when the Empire disappeared with "world power" in 1918. In the year of collapse and the thwarted restart, 1918–9, we found the immediate preconditions for the beginning of Hitler's political agitation, and thus of National Socialism. It is not a large jump to surmise that it was only in an extraordinary crisis of the kind that arose in 1918 that a social outsider would be able effectively to direct his warped and wounded soul outwards, in order to fulfil his "vocation" as a "politician" and, as happened, to evoke a response. His first successes were particularly in "popular cultural" circles of the type that had shaped his general "philosophy" before 1914. These, loaded with pseudo-scientific superstitions, delighted to advance a rag-bag of perverse imaginings in explanation of world history. Their imaginings stemmed from Social Darwinism, from popularized racial theories, from anti-Semitism and mystical conceptions of salvation, i.e. abstrusely perverted relics of the Christian doctrine of redemption. Hitler had absorbed all this during his youth in Vienna. From 1918 onwards, he made it the "philosophical" basis of his political agitation. Yet he differed in two respects from the type of "wandering scholars of popular culture whose positive achievement is always exactly zero", as Hitler himself said. His propaganda proposed a concrete political aim, the fight against Versailles, and it achieved its effectiveness by forceful campaigning with the aid of shock-troops and mass demonstrations.

Although Hitler's agitation had considerable success, in Bavaria at least, between 1920 and 1923, his "movement", even in the extreme situation of 1923, still lagged a long way behind the great "bourgeois" party of the right, the German Nationalists. This was certainly the consequence of Hitler's youthfulness, of numerous failings of the National Socialist German Workers' Party, of dilution by the large number of "popular" groups, of a lack of financial resources, and of much else besides. But most significant of all was the fact that the mass of voters who felt themselves to be "right-wing" were still too close to the unforgotten Empire, still too strongly bound to the symbol of the black, white and red flag, and still predominantly of such a "bourgeois" mentality that they were more deterred than attracted by swastika propaganda. Hitler's speeches and campaigning methods were not "bourgeois" and gave offence to the middle classes. However, he won over hardly any workers either, as these were to be found on the left, or within the Catholic Church. That people nevertheless joined him in consider-able numbers right at the beginning who were clearly neither bourgeoisie nor proletariat, was remarkable. They were not of any one social group. Much in evidence were those who stood apart from society or were not successful, who felt themselves unrecognized or who, mostly young men, were rebels against convention and the middle classes. But above all they were men who had become disorientated by the war and by the difficulties of adapting to the post-war years, or who felt excluded. Then there were youthful "idealists" who looked for fighting support at a time of national need and in face of the threat of revolution from the left, and thought they would best find it on the radical, "non-bourgeois" right. Thus there were many officers and students amongst the earliest "campaigners". The main mass of the increasing number of supporters and voters, however, were men of the lower middle class.

That "right-wing" and "national" could no longer be equated with "bourgeois" was something new, and at first it corresponded with the feeling of only a minority of the political right. But it was characteristic of many soldiers and officers who did not find their way into, or back into, middle-class life and who found accommoda-tion, and sought to perform their patriotic duty, first and foremost in the *Freikorps* (volunteer corps). Retrospective attempts have been made to characterize the attitude of these right-wing rebels, who had previously felt out of place on the right, as a "conservative revolution". The paradoxical nature of the phrase may reasonably reflect the confusion of this mood. These men were victims of the national crisis. They reacted to this crisis according to their origins, talents, experience and need in a way which for them resulted almost inevitably from the situation of 1919. Many of them joined

Hitler's party quickly, many held off because they did not wish to submit to Hitler's quickly apparent will to leadership, and many left the Party again, even before 1923, for this very reason. Then they remained the "homeless right" or "left-wingers of the right" and, as such, were of no use to Hitler.

After the turning-point of November 1923 when the *Reichsmark*, and with it the republic, were stabilized, Hitler lost many of his supporters at the time of his *Putsch* and brief imprisonment. In 1928, in the eyes of almost all Germans, he was nothing more than a ridiculous figure on the fringe of internal politics, and leader of a "splinter party" which was kept in existence by the party list election system of the republic. We have already established that this small party with its anti-Semitic ideology would probably have sunk further and further into oblivion if the great new crisis had not unexpectedly sent increasing masses of the type of people we have described flooding back to it.

The world economic crisis hit Germany and the United States harder than any other nation in the world. In the United States, the population reacted in accordance with the constitution in the Presidential elections of 1932 by voting out the Republicans, who had been in office since 1920, in the hope of salvaging reforms from Roosevelt. In Germany, no such escape route remained: the parliamentary system of government had proved unworkable in the governmental crisis leading to Brüning's appointment as Reichskanzler in March 1930, when no government with a working majority could be formed. When Brüning dissolved the Reichstag a few months later and had succumbed to the illusion of a successful appeal to the good sense of the electorate, in the spirit of the democratic conservative centre, fate intervened on 14 September 1930. The National Socialist Workers' Party became the party of the masses and rose from twelve to 107 seats in the Reichstag. The situation was different in America, where the constitution had been in use for a long time. In Germany the appeal to the voters led even further away from constitutional normality, until, on 31 July 1932, in another election, the National Socialists received over 37%, and the Communists over 14%, of the votes cast. With this negative majority that rejected the constitution itself the Reichstag became completely unworkable.

With this 37%, Hitler had reached the peak of his success in the terminal crisis of the Weimar Republic. After the Reichstag had been dissolved again immediately following its first assembly, the National Socialists lost two million votes in November 1932 and thus fell to 33% of the votes cast, while the other party of crisis, the German Communist Party, rose to 17%. This uneven movement of the two parties in the exploitation of the economic crisis before the end of the Republic can be attributed to several causes: to the tiring of the electorate, of whom a good 1.5 million fewer went to the polls than in July; to the acceptance of Chancellor von Papen's policy by conservatively minded voters, so that the German Nationalists regained a million votes and thus received 9% of the votes; further, to disappointment at the passivity of the Social Democratic Party, whose uninterrupted decline had continued since 1928 (in 1928 they had a bare 30%, in November 1932 a little over 20%). But a more fundamental factor lay behind all such specific reasons. The National Socialists and the Communists were, when we consider the mass influx of support, the dumping ground, so to speak, of the nationalist (especially liberal) bourgeoisie on the one hand, and the socialist proletariat on the other. But whereas the reservoir of the old parties from which these people defected was already drained as far as possible by the National Socialists, on the "Marxist" side it was still very much available in the mass of Social Democracy. Here there was only a gradual crumbling, and complete collapse could not be expected, even if there were a further continuation of the crisis. If the state successfully held out against the parties of crisis, then a falling-off of the crisis could be expected to produce a falling-off among the Communists and the National Socialists, for the very reason that both, especially the Communists, were less a party of the workers than a party of the workless.

This is an indication of the limits imposed upon Hitler as long as the nation enjoyed free expression of opinion. His agitation had remained ineffective, even at the time of his greatest successes, in the direction of the socialist left, whose two parties had shifted their balance only in relation to each other. Equally, he had made very few inroads into the Catholic parties of the centre and the Bavarian People's Party, who together had maintained their solid 15% from the period of the Empire. Meanwhile about half of the German National People's Party had proved capable of resistance. At their core were many loyal Protestants, many country people, and many who adhered to the "nationalist bourgeoisie" owing to a horror of Hitler's power to sway the masses and a fear of what might follow a "seizure of power". This horror and this fear were common to all those who deliberately voted against Hitler in 1932. That was two-thirds of the electorate, of whom, admittedly, only about 40% had voted for democratic parties. Agreement even amongst these did not extend very far. For the often expressed idea of an "emergency agreement" of all the democratic parties against the threat to their existence was not put into practice; and Chancellor Schleicher's last proposal to remedy the situation, made to the President in January 1933, to dissolve the Reichstag, to suspend elections for a while and to bridge the danger-period with a limited dictatorship, was not in accordance with the will of the parties, which were shortly afterwards delivered up to Hitler. Of these, the German Nationalists had already drawn closer to the National Socialist Workers' Party since the referendum against the Young Plan which they had arranged together with Hitler in 1929. National conservative politicians had far fewer inhibitions about National Socialism than about Social Democracy, the result of ten years of deterioration in relationships. Ideologically, this national right had much in common with National Socialism, as long as the latter's anti-Christian or racialist extravagances were not too much in evidence, as Hitler clearly wished. They were in agreement with Hitler in the fight against "Versailles" and against "Marxism". Most of all, however, Hitler's National Socialist Workers' Party, with its street-fighting groups, seemed the best protection against the danger, over-estimated at the time, of a Communist coup. Thus horror and fear of Hitler's mass movement amongst the conservatives were finally outweighed by false hopes.

If we look for the characteristics of that third of the nation which saw its saviour in Hitler in 1932, we see that the supporters of the National Socialist Workers' Party belonged mainly to the peasant and bourgeois "middle classes". Bitterness rose particularly high amongst the peasants, as they contracted increasing debts in the agricultural crisis, especially in Schleswig-Holstein and the eastern provinces. Small tradesmen had lost their savings in the inflation; they were hit hardest of all by the loss of purchasing power. Officials and employees were subjected to salary cuts, "need offerings", shorter working and unemployment. Young people bore the main brunt of this general collapse of living standards. They felt what it was to be "excluded", to have to live without employment or insurance and with reduced income. The careers they desired were closed to them; it was difficult or even impossible to start a family life. All this led young people to Hitler. Moreover, these fifteen- to thirty-year-olds were born in the years with the highest birth rates Germany had ever had, reaching a peak in 1910. This was expressed in the growth of the electorate by three millions between 1928 and 1932. But, however important the great crisis was as a factor in the massive increase in support of Hitler, deeper-lying characteristics of the electorate were equally important in aiding or hindering this growth. Most noteworthy is the fact that National Socialist gains were considerably fewer in Catholic than in Protestant constituencies. If secularized Protestantism had once favoured liberalism, it now turned rather towards National Socialism.

That National Socialism had the support of twelve to fourteen million people in the year 1932 may thus be seen largely as the result of destroyed security. However, it does not follow that these masses had adopted a nationalist, racialist and anti-Semitic *Weltanschauung*. They accepted such absurdities in passing and, without giving the matter much thought, probably imagined that there must be something in it, because Hitler must know. None of them had any idea what the consequences of this acceptance would turn out to be. What brought them together was lack of hope and complete loss of confidence in those who had "mismanaged" – formerly the "gentry" of the Empire, but now, and even more so, the "inferior" democrats; equally there was the "faith" bestowed upon the "Wonderman" and his work of salvation, whom people were ready to follow because there seemed no other hope, and because the threatening disintegration could only be averted by new discipline and order. All the disappointments of 1919 were once more alive. The fight against the *Diktat* of Versailles, which, together with the revolution of 1918, was seen as the cause and the beginning of deprivation, was still, in combination with the slogan "Freedom and Bread", Hitler's most popular demand. Stresemann's successes in foreign policy were ignored; only his failures, for example his vain wait for more rapid French co-operation, were fresh in the minds of these people, and Stresemann's phrase "a gleam of silver on the horizon" was held up to ridicule.

This, then, was the attitude of the twelve to fourteen millions of Hitler voters in 1932. Even the one million party members were mostly not to be regarded as faithful ideologues of National Socialist philosophy. They were, however, firmly convinced of the failure of the "November criminals" and of a future resurgence under Hitler's leadership.

After 30 January, when Hitler was formally appointed *Reichskanzler*, (but in reality "seized power"), the situation of the German people changed quickly, though in fact not, in the long run, as profoundly as it appeared. The parties and groups in opposition to Hitler gradually lost confidence in their own powers of resistance and in the possibility of resistance at all, as the power of the National Socialist leadership and its ruthless elimination of opposition grew stronger. Within only *one* year, the Germans of the Empire experienced the process of assimilation into a totalitarian power-structure, some with enthusiasm, unconcern and a hopeful sigh of relief, others with a sense of apprehension and helplessness. Success worked for Hitler. At the same time Mussolini's saying, that force creates agreement, proved correct. When all the political leaders who had stood apart from National Socialism were eliminated by their own recantations, or as martyrs, or allowed themselves to be brought into line, the impression was strengthened amongst the people that active resistance to Hitler's will was no longer possible. In the course of 1933 every German citizen had to grasp the new situation: the only political possibility remaining was the National Socialist leadership of the Empire. Even the conservative illusion that Hitler could be more or less held down in a coalition with men like Papen and Hugenberg was quickly dispelled. The National Socialist Workers' Party and the State fused into a unity, or, in other words, the party, in obedience to the Führer, disposed of the state, without counterbalance or control. The nation was delivered over to Hitler but believed, or was maintained in the belief, that Hitler was "its" man, a son of the people, elected by the people, concerned for the welfare of the people, and a saviour in their time of trouble, who would lead them to new greatness.

As there were very soon outward successes, in particular the quick drop in unemployment – partly because the crisis was on the wane, partly as a result of drastic works programmes – the wave of National Socialist influence by suggestion rose quickly in 1933 and reached, even if to a mixed and limited extent, considerable numbers of that half of the people who still remained aloof after the Reichstag elections of 5 March.

Outside the area of the Reich, National Socialist penetration, which had only been weak before 1933, similarly strengthened, chiefly but not exclusively in the areas directly adjacent to the enclosed area of settlement. This sharpened the contentious situation of the Germans within the ethnic groups of eastern central Europe, described above. The latter saw the German Reich rising to new and obvious greatness. At the same time their confidence in the permanence of the European system of 1919 was eroded, and their mistrust of the frontier settlements of the peace treaties was increased. On the other hand, the emergence of open or disguised National Socialist organizations amongst the Germans in the eastern central European states caused a division among the ethnic groups which was demoralizing and destructive. The aggressive leaders of the so-called "Renewal Movements" sharply attacked the experienced politicians of the ethnic groups who had always worked by a combination of assertion and compromise. Their attacks were made mainly in the hope that the National Socialist German Reich would soon intervene decisively, directly or indirectly, in the states of eastern central Europe. The majority of "ethnic Germans", however, adopted a reticent attitude to these "renewers", partly from the instinctive feeling that in an alien environment they could not afford to risk endangering even further their home and their cultural freedom, and partly from a rejection of National Socialism, mostly by reason of church membership.

Whereas free differences of opinion between Germans were still possible in the ethnic groups, the Germans in the Reich grew accustomed to the increasing elimination of opposition in all areas of life, that is to total, all-pervasive politicization on rigid lines. Of course, the mature socialists, conservatives and the last of the convinced liberal democrats, especially active Catholics and Protestants, did not lose their old roots. They remained what they had been, far more than appearances indicated; and there were many underground circles in which the spirit of resistance was kept alive, even if open resistance was not possible. But what could be done in practice? The question of what the politicians of the dissolved parties had done when there was still time, before they had been rendered powerless, was an embarrassing one. For the great majority of people who had not emigrated and who had no wish to be put in a concentration camp, there was no other alternative than to adapt, as people in similar freedom-denying systems do to this day. Even in the working class, adaptation became common, although resistance here had been clearly greater than in other professional groups. This could be seen in elections for works councils, which were soon suspended because of their unfavourable results. If, as has not yet been done, the process of adaptation within the working class were to be examined, in so far as this would be possible with the probable lack of source material, a clear difference between the generations would emerge. The "excluded" young people of before 1933, who now found employment either again or for the first time, had, understandably, a different attitude to their unquestionably improved situation than the old workers who had grown up in the working-class movement, whose trade unions had been ruthlessly smashed, and who remained predominantly suspicious as a result of long experience.

At the beginning of 1933 civil servants also streamed into the party while membership remained open; members of the intelligentsia, who had been only sparsely represented amongst the "old campaigners", made themselves available in large numbers; this, not to mention the compulsory enrolment of students, accounts for the successful National Socialist captures of 1933. Not only were the usual totalitarian methods applied, a mixture of revolutionary fervour, intimidation and propaganda, but now the whole weight of the state and its tradition were thrown in. From now on, loyalty to the government and service of the state, such as had always been given, were to be bound up with affirmation of, and adherence to, National Socialism. The civil servant must no longer separate party and state. Many submitted to this demand, whether from conviction, from fear, or for the sake of their careers. Many only gave the appearance of doing so, or even refused to join the Party. By doing so they entered a permanent situation of conflict which could one day expose them to serious danger. The problem of officers was different from that of civil servants, as they were excluded from party membership. The usual exclusion from politics (after Seeckt) was maintained and conceded by Hitler in practice, to some extent even after the intervention of 1938. Thus, for many of the Army, there was a possibility of living cocooned in a kind of inner emigration, although opportunities for this were offered most clearly by subordinate positions in business life.

However, just as the Army in practice played along, however great its reservations were, particularly those of the senior officers, so did the whole nation, whatever the individual grievances or resistance. There seemed to be no cracks in the outwardly gleaming façade. The gauges of success were impressive; nor did they miss their effect abroad. On the day of Potsdam, on 23 March 1933, the old Prussian-German tradition, reassuringly for many, seemed to merge into the young revolution of the nation; Hitler bowed deeply to the old Field Marshal. On 1 May 1933, of which the celebrations in Berlin have been impressively described by François-Poncet, the deploying people's community seemed to have left the class struggle behind. On 17 May of the same year, Hitler made his famous peace speech in the Reichstag, and its great lie sounded so honest that it had considerable effect at home and abroad. Long might the chain of events or successes continue, in which the nation, as a community of achievement and of purpose, seemed to stand with unanimous conviction behind Hitler's leadership! It was only necessary to remember the motorways, the creation of employment, the treaty of friendship with Poland (which seemed to be a courageous step towards the settlement of the, till then, contentious east), the return to the Saarland, the reintroduction of military conscription, the occupation of the Rhineland (demilitarized since the Peace Treaty), the Olympic Games in Berlin, the evidence of German-British friendship in the naval agreement with Great Britain, and much else. In great parades and demonstrations on public holidays, mostly recently introduced National Socialist ones, the unity of Führer and people, as it seemed, found powerful expression.

But the chain of successful events could meanwhile be matched by a chain of horrific events, and even the chain of successes did not lack horror. To be remembered is the "Presidential Decree for the Protection of People and State", issued in connection with the Reichstag fire on 28 February 1933, which granted powers to suspend a number of important basic rights, then the Enabling Act and the permanent state of emergency which followed, the reign of terror against the Jews that began as early as 1933, the unleashing of the battle with the churches, the murders after Hitler's coup against Röhm, and much besides.

From 1933 on, the Germans of the Reich were in a constant state of attraction or repulsion, often both at the same time. They reacted very differently, according to their political convictions before 1933 or to newly significant biological accident. With reference to those who had opposed the National Socialists before 1933, and also disappointed old comrades of the National Socialist Workers' Party, the view expressed occasionally, that Germany was the first country in Europe to be occupied by the National Socialists, may be taken *cum grano salis*. However, German realities from 1933 to 1944 match neither the picture of a National Socialist occupation nor the façade of 99% compulsory obedience of the nation to the will of the Führer. Both thoroughgoing National Socialists and immune opponents were minorities. Most Germans were not "heroes", either of the National Socialist revolution or of resistance to it. That was normal and human.

The true believers found themselves in a minority. Naturally, their number did not correspond with the old core of the early days before mass membership. Many of the old campaigners had become cynical nihilists, if they had not been such from the beginning. On the other hand many young people had come along unspoiled, especially from the Hitler Youth. But even in that very movement, initiation into the workings of National Socialism often led to mere routine or even to wastage, the further the twelve-year period advanced. There is a direct, mental link between the Hitler Youth and the "sceptical generation" of the first decade after the war.

Initiation and wastage soon came more and more to replace the genuine or contrived fervour of the "national revolution" of 1933. They were the expression of resignation or, even more, of unthinking acceptance. The feeling that revolt was senseless was probably one of the most profound effects, even after-effects of National Socialism. Yet this meant that human, moral resistance was no longer summoned up, because it was all in vain, and that, on the contrary, scepticism, cynicism and amoral opportunism were created or provoked. It led to the practices characteristic of all such political systems: wriggling out, keeping a low profile, sly deceit, seeking advantage from the prospects offered by an amoral world, where living a permanent two-faced lie is unavoidable. Not the least part of this was living as far as possible without noticing injustice and outrage. It was best to know as little as possible of this, so that the conscience was not burdened, and involvement in misfortune did not become unbearable. For the rest, most saw in the harsh tensions of war only what concerned them directly: service and battle at the front, work in the operation and management of the war, release of tension and periods of good living when there was the opportunity, the fear of bombing raids, despair and sorrow at the death of those close. How far was it possible to think beyond personal concerns?

But it would be unjust to end here our judgement of the moral effect of National Socialism upon the German people. For it was National Socialism which reawakened old moral forces of great strength in a double, extremely ambiguous way, which it is important to remember:

1. In the name of the people's community, which was naïvely and honestly believed by most people to be what the name said, without its value to Hitler's world war strategy being realized, many people demonstrated a readiness for sacrifice of a level which is not often or easily shown by human beings of their own free will. It became a popular idea that, after years of privation, the common task was to reconstruct the nation with a sense of service and joyfully accepted duty. This was linked up with comradeship at the front in the world war. "If I survive, what's that to me, as long as the Fatherland is free", sang the Hitler Youth. Langemarck became even more of a legend than in the twenties. In the German army from 1939 to 1942, to some extent even to the bitter end, a spirit of sacrifice that matched the song and the legend lived on, even if both these faded before the harsh realities of the front and the solitariness of the soldier exposed between life and death. Certainly, terrible misuse was made of this spirit of sacrifice in pursuance of Hitler's plans of conquest and extermination. But this cannot alter the fact that most German soldiers were simply not aware of this connection, and many of them, alive or dead, passed the final test of the extreme face-to-face situation in a way that silences all retrospective disparagement. The power to overcome naked egoism was immeasurably great in the war, not only in the form of bravery in face of the enemy, but no less in selfless human support of neighbours, both at the front and amidst the privations at home. This touches upon a general human characteristic, the readiness, which always appears in exceptional circumstances, to see beyond the simple instinct for self-preservation and to aid the weak who are in direct need of help. That specific sense of allegiance to any one national community, which is common to peoples everywhere who believe their national unity is in danger of dissolution, under attack or in need of defence, also lasted well into the war. This was largely the way in which National Socialism was perceived. It was the view of credulous people who could not grasp the implications of the ideology and reality of Hitler's policies.

2. The other, even more difficult test, one refined by conscious internal decision, which was provoked, unwanted, by National

Socialism, was that of active resistance, with personal involvement, at the risk of one's own life. Here, moral strength was demanded comparable with that of soldiers at the front. Only it was even greater, because the decision in favour of active resistance was not the naturally inbred, generally approved, readiness for sacrifice in the old tradition of dying for one's country; first it had to be decided whether resistance, to the extent of assassination of the Head of the Reich and of the Army, was really justified. Men came together in active resistance whose consciences had refused to be blunted and drove them to act, not out of subjective caprice but according to an objective and universal moral law. As there was no official opposition in the state, they had to seek other ways of freeing the German people, and the conquered peoples, from a diabolical regime, to which could be applied the words of the Bible, "Ye ought to obey God rather than men." It may be seen as an illustration of a widespread change amongst responsible thinkers that Count Stauffenberg, who made a bomb attack upon the tyrant on 20 July 1944, had enthusiastically welcomed Hitler's national revolution, as a lieutenant in uniform at the head of a large crowd, on 30 January 1933.

Both of these, the fighting of the soldiers at the front and the active resistance to Hitler, had their effect, in the Hitler era and beyond, upon the shaping and the cohesion of the German nation of the future. In both, a spirit which (in the army) was not primarily National Socialist or (in the resistance) in deliberate contrast to Hitler's ideology, gave expression to a demand which Hitler wore threadbare by his concept of a "popular community" when agitating for *his* interpretation of the word. The concept was in use long before Hitler and quite simply indicates the fact that in a modern nation, without the estates system, all men in a national democracy are members or parts of a common whole. Hitler reinterpreted the concept, which had admitted a diversity in unity, and tried to eliminate diversity and independence in favour of co-ordinated, directed uniformity. The nation did come together in practice for Hitler as a great community of achievement, that is, in unity, to the extent of the sacrifice of men and women in the total war. But the same nation remained, more than it appeared, a nation of diversity and will to human independence. This was so at the front, where character and achievement were demanded, and not National Socialist views. There was no catch-word for this spirit, as it worked its way into the difficult period of the primitive new beginning, unlike after 1918, when all too frequent use had been made of *Frontgeist* (the spirit of the trenches).

No less far-reaching in its effects was the "popular community" of the resistance fighters. In 1937 the Bishop of Berlin, Count von Preysing, declared: "Never before . . . have we been so deeply united in love and compassion with our brothers who differ from us in their faith". In this he expressed a mood highly characteristic of the resistance to Hitler. The threat to humans, by the tyrannies of the inhuman, forced together those who knew they were united in concern for the basic values of human existence. This was the way it happened, as the Bishop confirmed, with Catholics and Protestants. But the unifying power of such an alliance went far beyond the solidarity of the Church. Conservatives, liberals, trade-unionists and socialists came together, all of whom had been separated before 1933 and not prepared to come to an emergency understanding. They drew their conclusions from the experiences they had had to undergo since 1933. They had learned that everything that had separated them before had been of little significance in the political existence of the nation compared with that which separated them from the crushing tyranny. So, in small groups, with the intention of expanding later, they created a popular community that had been forced upon them by Hitler. The effects of this spread beyond 1945 into the early years of the Federal Republic. Only the communists, many of whom had been drawn in, often by concentration camp friendships, split off again after 1945, as they were not permitted to recognize diversity of freedom within national unity.

From the beginning, the relationship between National Socialism and the German nation was not merely an internal question which the Germans could have settled amongst themselves. Since Hitler had already demanded the quick removal of the "fetters of Versailles" before 1933, his assumption of government had to cause partly concern and partly anticipation within the states of Europe. To take the first opportunity of military intervention in order to pre-empt the danger was far from the minds of the victorious powers of the world war. Instead of this they hoped first for caution, then for restraint on the part of Hitler. Until the Munich Agreement on 30 September 1938, a Europe split four ways, into a community of political interest of Great Britain, France, Germany and Italy, did not seem to be impossible, in spite of all the impediments to this idea occasioned by the violent methods of Hitler and Mussolini. A section of the eastern European states, especially Poland, Hungary and Yugoslavia, even tried to share in Hitler's successes, so that there were many prospects in the eastern European crisis zone for an energetic German policy of revision. Intensive bilateral economic relations, especially between Germany and the south-east European countries, were advantageous for both sides.

If, in spite of the apparently favourable course of Hitler's revisionist policy, which was at first hesitant and then vigorous, there was much serious concern abroad even before 1938, this was not without good reason. One of the most important factors was the treatment of the Jews in Germany, which clearly showed that Hitler intended to take his anti-Semitism and the corresponding paragraph of the party programme seriously. Through the "Reich Citizenship Law" and the "Law for the Protection of German Blood and German Honour" of the year 1935, all Jews were expressly excluded from the German nation, to which they had belonged since the Emancipation Laws of the early nineteenth century. No Jew could be a "citizen of the Reich"; marriages "between Jews and nationals of German or kindred stock" were forbidden. "Racial separation" was made increasingly effective in grossly offensive forms, in schools, for example. Even before the beginning of open violence, therefore, and the burning of the synagogues, the looting, and the final exclusion of the Jews from economic life in November 1938, the sharp incision had been made. The nation was condemned to part from its people of Jewish origin, who had flowed in during the course of a century, bringing not only wealth to the economy, but above all a wealth of 'intelligence and talent to scientific and cultural life. Certainly their assimilation had not gone on without conflict, especially in the early days of emancipation, when it became clear that there could be no uniform solution to the question of how far the Jews should remain a racial and religious community in spite of emancipation, and thus remain a nation in themselves, or whether they should be completely assimilated; moreover, the process of absorption was, in any case, disturbed by a sudden, strong influx of Jews from eastern central Europe immediately after 1918. But, on the whole, the nation had been enriched by German-Jewish symbiosis, in spite of unavoidable frictions, and anti-Semitism, which can be seen as a waste-product of the old Christian-Jewish antagonism following on secularization and emancipation, had been

no stronger in Germany than in many other countries of the world.
The forcible separation of Jews from Germans was an immeasurably
huge and painful operation. In the years from 1933 till the prohibition of emigration in 1941, about 300,000 out of a total of half a
million German Jews emigrated. What this meant to the position of
the German nation in the world, especially in the USA, can hardly
be over-estimated.

As in general in international politics, so also in the Jewish
question many hopes remained alive, and many illusions in the air,
until well into 1938. After the synagogue fires on 8–9 November
1938 and the occupation of Prague on 15 March 1939, however,
such hopes and illusions finally vanished. The German nation,
which was Hitler's to command, and whose will was his will, had
finally lost the opportunity to unite with the western powers in face
of the Soviet Russian threat, a policy introduced by Stresemann,
and even clearly carried on at first under Hitler. Instead of this, the
nation now stood isolated between East and West, and only other
"have-nots" like the over-populated powers, Italy and Japan, a few
eastern central European satellites and enemies of England or Jewry
in the Near East, had any degree of sympathy for German policy.
This was already the line-up for the Second World War, which was
only temporarily held up by the shared politicking of the German-
Soviet Pact of 1939.

Earlier, in an even more favourable line-up, Hitler achieved, by
the pressure of an ultimatum in 1938, the occupation of and thus
union with Austria and the German-settled border areas of Bohemia
and Moravia, the so-called Sudetenland, which had altogether
around ten million Germans of the former Habsburg monarchy. Of
course, these were acts of violence, which were later recognized as
preliminaries to further expansion and the domination of eastern
Europe (the *Ostraum*). But they were accepted and recognized by
the western powers, as their will to prevent them was not strong
enough, and they were felt to be bound up with the refusal of the
right of self-determination in 1919, a feeling that was particularly
strong in England. The joy of the German population of Austria
and of the Sudetenland was great and genuine. The revision of the
unjust peace treaties of Versailles and St. Germain was completed.
Nevertheless, these outwardly splendid days of the double union
had evil consequences. For it was, in fact, less union after a just
reparation of omissions of 1919 than the beginning of a chain of

events leading to the new world war. And moreover, especially in Austria and to a lesser extent in the Sudetenland, the National Socialists encountered a country whose people did still, as they had in 1919, desire unification with the German Reich, but who were not, apart from a minority, inclined to submit to National Socialism. Neither the socialists, who had been suppressed since 1933 by Dollfuss's amendment to the constitution, nor the Christian Socialists, who were linked with the Catholic Church, agreed to fall in with National Socialism for the sake of union. Thus it inevitably happened that, up to the end in 1945, the dictatorship of the National Socialists, who were by no means only Reich Germans but rather predominantly natives, and in particular SS action against the Church, created so much bitterness in the country that the once unifying idea of a greater Germany fell into disrepute. The renewed transition to "independence" in 1945, therefore, seemed to many to be a liberation, a different situation from 1919, even if the desire amongst the population for separation from Germany was by no means a foregone conclusion. The Sudeten Germans in 1945, however, were given no opportunity to come to terms with a new Czechoslovakia, as they were dispossessed and driven from their homeland.

In the Second World War events came to light which, up until then, had mostly been regarded as impossible both inside and outside Germany. With frightful consistency, Hitler attempted to achieve the aims he had published as a young man in 1925 in *Mein Kampf:* the conquest of a wide area of eastern Europe (*Ostraum*) and the annihilation of all Jews who came into his clutches. He had never revoked the contents of this book, but these passages were generally regarded as mere brainstorms, which could no longer apply to the responsible, instinctively sure statesman. Within our terms of reference, it has little purpose to enquire whether, and to what extent, Hitler did in fact keep both these "final aims" permanently in mind in the years before the war. Nevertheless, the new world war presented him with extreme opportunities and he was ruthless to exploit them. In doing so, he brought misapplication of the German national community of achievement to its gruesome conclusion. The German nation, strengthened by the "kindred" smaller Germanic peoples, was allegedly called to rule the "inferior" Slav peoples, who were therefore only of value as tools. Whilst these peoples were to be deprived of their own leaders and of access to higher culture and education, the east, far into Russia, was to be ruled by means of German-Germanic administrative and defence centres. Above all, Hitler's SS stood by to create the conditions for this policy. This was not only more than, but something entirely different from, the idea of the political large-scale concern "Central Europe" in the First World War. It was, even after an (impossible) German victory, entirely unrealistic, but above all it meant the completely ruthless suppression, exploitation and elimination of the élites of other peoples.

All this was only exceeded by the so-called "final solution" of the Jewish question, which was decided upon in 1941 and carried on until the very last months of the war with mass killings speeded by technical processes. What happened in Auschwitz and other camps far exceeds, in its methodical mass extermination, all the other outrages of the modern world, which is well equipped for such purposes. In contrast to the plans for Eastern Europe, this rapid "final solution" was, in the long term, not unrealistic. The vast majority of Jews in central and eastern Europe met a frightful death. It was ordered by the "leader" of the German nation, whose last words to his people, amidst the ruins of Berlin on 29 April 1945, were a call to resistance against "international Jewry". This *idée fixe* had remained the central idea in his *Weltanschauung*. It had hardly been considered by the masses who had helped him to "power" from 1930 to 1933; they had either accepted it or had pushed it aside as embarrassing. But now the nation was loaded down for the future by the outrages of a man who escaped all personal consequences by suicide.

IX THE PARTITIONED NATION
IN THE DIVIDED WORLD

In 1945 Germany was a heap of rubble. To many it seemed to be the end of the German nation. And yet, from the very first day after the cease-fire onwards, it was also a new beginning that was not without confidence. The heap of rubble, the end, and the new beginning of 1945 still have direct influence today, although the rubble has disappeared, history has moved on, and the new beginning has disappointed initial expectations.

It was not only the bombed-out towns with their wealth of economic power and their traditions of art and culture that lay in ruins. National Socialism, with its ruthlessness and its talk of a "thousand year" Reich, also lay in ruins. The Allies occupied the whole of Germany and divided it into zones of occupation. They took away from the Germans any authority of their own, and thus, also, responsibility for a settlement of accounts with the twelve years of the "Third Reich". The Allies forced upon the Germans the procedure of the questionnaire, which led millions of those who completed one to conceal, or play down, as much as possible of what was now regarded as "criminal". As a bad classification was attended by disadvantages or punishment, much had now to be "forgotten", or reinterpreted a little. For who would willingly accept these unnecessarily, especially when the procedure was imposed by foreign victors? The political lie on an individual level, which had just been escaped, continued therefore under the opposite sign. These were bad psychological conditions for the efforts at "re-education" instigated particularly by the Americans. "Denazification" and democratic re-education from outside would probably have remained unsuccessful, and would even have produced a violent defensive reaction, if the policy had not, in general, been battering at an open door. The longer National Socialist rule had lasted, and the more fearfully the war had deteriorated, the more extensive had been the process of erosion mentioned earlier. From 1930 to 1933, millions upon millions had gone over to Hitler; the period of early successes seemed, if certain doubts were ignored, to confirm their hopes. But when it came to war, and when the war, especially after 1941, seemed to become more and more pointless and to demand more and more sacrifices, it was only natural that the influx during the period of crisis and hope around 1932 should be replaced by a corresponding exodus – even if, to outward appearances, all remained in good order under the sign of the swastika. The fires of enthusiasm and confidence were long extinguished in most Germans when collapse came into sight, when the foreign armies occupied the country and the military governments of the victors were set up. With a feeling of complete impotence, which was also physically painful because there had to be hunger too, the last embers of a once great fire went out; a heap of ashes remained. In so far as there was strength left at all for more than preoccupation with bare existence, some still felt bound by their old party allegiances, whilst others turned away in disappointment and resignation and thus brought in the "not with me" (*ohne mich*) attitude to all politics, which remained widespread for many years. Many former National Socialists also took refuge in the "not with me" attitude; it goes without saying that they developed an emotional attitude both to the victorious powers and the newly re-emerging German administrative, and later governing, authorities; but this attitude produced no new, active political will; all that remained was a retreat into private bitterness and, in the course of the years, the satisfaction of being able to play a part in small-scale attempts at grouping round extreme right-wing parties or newspapers. From all this, however, nothing has emerged till now which could in any way be called significant, either in intellectual stature or in its effects in wider circles, or even amongst young people. How fundamentally different it had all been in the years after 1919, when the Right was really on the move and it was, above all, young people who had kept the movement alive!

Thus National Socialism has been extinct among the German people since 1945. There is still an "Old Nazism" which is dying out by natural process, but no "Neo-Nazism", although this spectre has been summoned up over and over again, partly for reasons of political insinuation and partly from defective understanding of historical and political realities.

The after-life of National Socialism amongst the Germans can be understood to some extent from the experience of a generation. If it is true that men are shaped mainly by the constraints, happenings and experience of their youth between the ages of fifteen and twenty-five, then those who were "scarred" by Versailles are only to be found in those over seventy, those shaped by the crisis of democracy in 1930 only amongst those over sixty. But many of those who today are younger than sixty underwent their decisive experiences before 1933. They may still partly have been under the spell of the short years of National Socialist growth, but, more than that, they experienced in themselves the process of erosion, and for those over fifty today their generation's experience of the final struggle, collapse and smoking ruins may have remained decisive. But young people today are remote even from that generation shattered by 1945. It is worthwhile to reflect upon this declining effect of the major scars of 1919, 1930–3 and 1945 within the age-distribution of the present-day nation. In this, National Socialism is to a certain extent limited by, at one end, the elderly and very old, whose spiritual and intellectual roots go back to the period before 1930, indeed some even partly before 1919, and who therefore had to spring into the political breach in 1945, and at the other end by young people and infants who either have only a small awareness of the collapse of 1945, or who no longer, except through parents or school, have any link at all with the destiny of the nation before 1945.

After the Germans had taken their affairs more and more back into their own hands, it became possible to conduct an examination of the National Socialist past a little more openly. Nevertheless, this has still not developed to the point of uninhibited freedom. After all that has happened, that is not humanly possible. It is equally impossible to "overcome" the past.

The most difficult question in the post-1945 examination of National Socialism is that of guilt. If more had been known inside and outside Germany about guilt and atonement in the Christian sense, the accusation of "collective guilt" would have been disposed of more quickly. Only an individual sins, not a collective. Then it could equally clearly have been said of the judging authority that guilty men can only stand before human judges where this is demanded by clear evidence according to valid laws. Seen from this point of view, much that was practised legally or was expressed in judgement by "public opinion" after 1945 was highly questionable. This is not to play down the full frightfulness of what had happened, either in the cases in which justice had to be done in accordance with the law, or in the many cases in which there was no legally valid evidence, but where the individual had to make his own judgement, in his conscience, about how he became enmeshed in guilt. As this enmeshment affected many, however, and finally the whole nation, the question of guilt does finally extend beyond the individual case and points at the nation as a whole, without this being "collective guilt"; for this nation had gone to meet its destiny with almost all its members actively engaged. This has often been pointed out, even in the Hitler period itself. From this, for the Christian, there follows the necessity of penance, that is to say, of active conversion.

Goerdeler closed his farewell letter from prison with the words: "But I beg the world to accept our martyrs' fate as a penance for the German people." Many thought like this in the resistance. Therein lay, and lies, the deepest significance of 20 July 1944. But such a conception of the relationship of guilt and atonement is far removed from all those who, as members of other nations, self-righteously pass judgement upon a people whose national character is supposedly irredeemably evil, or those within the nation who lightly regard all attempts to take guilt and atonement seriously as harmful self-laceration. Where the boundary lies between hard searching of the conscience and destructive self-mutilation is a question that can only be decided by reference to individual responsibility. While the first goes on in silence, the second is public and thus unavoidably exposed to political misuse by those who have an interest in the self-accusation of their opponents.

Even in earlier times, it was human to avoid acknowledgement of guilt and need for penance. How much more so in our era of declining Christian influence in public and private life! The Germans are no different in this from the other nations of "western civilization". Furthermore, it must be said that it has truly not been made easy since 1945 for the Germans to face the horror of their recent past openly and without inhibition, without dogmatic defensiveness on the one hand or modish assiduity on the other.

The year of the heap of rubble was also the end of much with which Germans of today's older generation grew up as a natural part of life. First, it brought the end, in practice if not in international law, of the German east – not only of most of the ethnic groups and language islands of eastern central Europe but also of the old Prussian provinces east of the Oder and the Neisse, from which the population were almost entirely expelled. This was an inhuman response to Hitler's plans for eastern Europe, which arose from Russian expansion to the west and the enforced driving of Poland westwards, whilst the Germans of the eastern language islands had already largely been given the impetus to leave their homeland by Hitler's resettlement treaties with the Soviet Union. The Germans were driven almost completely out of the eastern part of Europe, and thus a fundamentally new situation was created in Europe. It is true that German ethnic groups in south-east Europe, especially in Rumania (Transylvania), reformed after heavy losses due to death and deportation. But these are poor remnants. Compared with the earlier position, the Germans in eastern central Europe have almost sunk into insignificance. Even more incisive is the violent end of German life in the old German-Czech cultural communities of Bohemia and Moravia, together with the loss of the rich provinces east of the Oder and the Görlitz Neisse with the ports of Memel, Königsberg, Elbing, Danzig and Stettin, and the old universities of Königsberg and Breslàu. What has here been lost to the nation as a whole cannot be measured in population figures and economic statistics. Until 1970 it remained an open question in international law to which state those German eastern provinces would finally be assigned which had been placed temporarily "under the administration of the Polish state until the final settlement of Poland". The ruling was postponed because a peace treaty with Germany after 1945 was never signed. The western Allies opposed their *de facto* incorporation by the Poles, who were supported by the Soviet Union and the German Democratic Republic. Until 1970 the government of the Federal Republic of Germany maintained its legal claim that the boundaries of Germany in 1937 should provide the basis in international law for peace negotiations.

In 1945, not only was the German east lost, but the end had also come of the German Reich or the German national state. From the initial situation of "supreme authority" exercised by four military governments there emerged in practice after 1949 two German states divided by the "Cold War" front, whilst Austria had already been separated off again in 1945.

Seven years of National Socialist restriction of liberty, together with the fact of being drawn into the vortex of the German catastrophe, had brought about in Austria what had not been reached in two decades of undesired "independence" from 1918 to 1938. Separation from Germany – where was Germany? – was now complete, welcomed by some, accepted with resignation by others. Austria enjoyed the advantage of being regarded as a "liberated" rather than an "enemy" country and thus could immediately be constituted as a state in 1945. It is true that Austria continued to be occupied for some years by the four principal Allied powers, but partition was avoided, a state treaty was signed in 1955 between the Allies and Austria, after long difficulties, and her neutrality in international law was recognized by both east and west. In the dangerous conditions of the Cold War, all this was a favourable development. It is an indication of the way the overall situation had fundamentally changed in relation to the twenties that this course of events was accepted. Today the idea of union has become outmoded. The independence of the federal Austrian state is seen as permanent on both sides of the frontier. In 1848, the German Austrians had still belonged to the German Confederation, and yet the Austrian federation, with its nationalities and its countries which lay outside the German Confederation, could not be united with Germany. Greater Germany had remained an unfulfilled aspiration. In 1866–71, the severance was made between little Germany and greater Austria, and in 1918 little Germany became a national democratic republic, while a German-Austrian republic was formed out of the collapse of greater Austria. Now the hour had struck for a democratic greater Germany in the spirit of 1848, and with the black, red and gold symbol of 1848. But this was thwarted by the peace treaties. When greater Germany was brought into existence by force twenty years later by Hitler, and compelled to live under the sign of the swastika, it was also condemned to pass away with Hitler. In consequence, the German-Austrian republic was released in the collapse of the German Reich and was severed as a political entity from its links with the two great areas in its history, on the one hand Germany, on the other the Danube area.

In this connection, two things may be expected in the future: a lasting connection with the German nation and a continuing decline

in the importance of frontiers in a future Europe. Neither contradicts
the independence of the state or the historically shaped character of
Austria. But both are of a kind to free Austria from the danger of
narrowness and to restore that breadth and generous scale which
have marked her history in connection with Germany and south-
eastern Europe. The period in her past from 1918 to 1945 still rests
heavily on Austria. In the east, she is shut off from the Danube area
by the "Iron Curtain". In relation to Germany, however, official
Austria, as a consequence of a certain reaction to *Anschluss* and of
the attempt to create a "national" ideology of her own, is still not
sufficiently uninhibited to bring about a German mutuality that
fully respects state frontiers. Even to the south, the view across the
frontier is not unclouded, as the question of South Tyrol still raises
difficulties in spite of the Austrian-Italian agreement of 1946 which
brought a settlement in principle. In 1945 Austria had made a vain
attempt to reincorporate the German-settled area of Tyrol, which
had been allocated to Italy in 1919 because of the Brenner frontier.
Thus, South Tyrol has remained a relic of the Europe of nationality
struggles after the First World War.

Otherwise, however, this Europe of 1919 has passed away, and
there can be absolutely no more talk of a European state system.
The former allies against Hitler, the Americans and the Russians,
took up hostile positions in the middle of Europe and have retained
them to the present day. That is to say, Europe, like Germany, has
been partitioned since 1945. Eastern-central Europe, apart from the
special case of Yugoslavia, has been forced into the block of Russian
communist states, as it was occupied by the Russian army towards
the end of the war and has not been released again since. That in a
position like this after 1945 a political movement developed in
western Europe with the aim of an "integrated" or "federated"
Europe is an indication not only of the historically based power of
the European idea but even more of the related necessity to form
large units in modern technical and economic conditions. However
far Europe is realized in the future beyond the present partial
successes in western Europe, this much is certain, that the time of a
self-contained system of European states, which believed itself to be
the centre of the world, and even *was* this for a time, has passed.
The catastrophe of the Second World War meant a deep incision in
the history of Europe: the end of the old links and a new beginning
in completely changed conditions. That is also fundamental to

Germany's new beginning.

If this beginning in the new world situation of the atomic age is to be fully understood, the memory of what ended in 1945 must first be rounded off. The German catastrophe of that year was the painful end of the national revolutionary movement of the German nation. Let us look back once more. The German national movement had prepared itself as an idea towards the end of the eighteenth century, and had been politically challenged by the foreign domination of Napoleon; from then on it had not come to rest, since the German question, as we have seen, never found a satisfactory solution in a national state, even in 1871 only to an incomplete extent. As a consequence of the peace treaties of 1919, the disparity between on the one hand the desired ideal solution of a national state, in accordance with the right to self-determination, and on the other hand the post-war order that was established against this desire, had become so great that violent nationalist feeling became inevitable. We have seen that Hitler had found a platform for his first successes in this emotional atmosphere of 1919. But there is no direct, "necessary" path leading from "Versailles" to the "seizure of power". For as early as the twenties there had been visible, in hopeful initiatives, the possibility of a lasting settlement, and the incorporation of Germany into an international system of "collective security". In the longer view, compromise solutions seemed to be attainable, in which Germany would defer, but where, on the other hand, German desires for revision would also be acceded to. Not only the policies of German governments but also the mood of the vast majority of the German nation-state were directed towards this end. Just how slight support was for defiant national reactions in international politics had been indicated in 1929 by the referendum and plebiscite against the Young Plan, which had obtained only 10% and 14% of the possible vote. But in the vortex of the world economic crisis, this move towards the sensible incorporation of Germany and German co-operation in international peace-keeping had been interrupted, and the Germans devoted themselves once more, voluntarily or involuntarily, to the aim of delivering the counterblow to "1919" by their own means, in defiance of all opposition; in the course of this they inadvertently became the instrument of the dreams of dominion of a hybrid conqueror. With this, however, the wave of national revolution and national presumption collapsed and turned into spray. Clearly it was finally exhausted. All national slogans of the reascent of sovereign German power by its own means fell silent, and where they are still voiced amongst relics, they have a ridiculous phantom effect and are no longer accepted by the sobered nation.

This is not only the result of abhorrence of the National Socialist perversion of the German national movement, for such abhorrence could weaken in the change of a generation. It is rather that time has run out for every kind of national revolutionary presumption and national self-glorification. That this is understood with such particular clarity by Germans of today is accounted for to a large extent by the experiences of the ill-fated National Socialist experiment. In the nineteenth century, the aim of creating a sovereign national state, strong through the national economy and capable of self-defence – and at the same time the state of a great people – was sensible and appropriate to the age. That had already become debatable in the era of the two world wars. Since the explosion of the first atom bomb it has become meaningless. It is not only for Germany that the reality of the politically and militarily independent national state has come to an end.

The nation amongst nations has, however, remained. Since 1945, that has been forcibly proved everywhere on earth. Nations, however, even the great ones, have acquired a fundamentally different status in the political order and disorder of the world. For the Germans, this change coincided with the catastrophic end of their national state. In no other great nation, therefore, has the break in continuity, and thus with its own history, been so great as it has with the Germans. Their new beginning as a nation amongst nations in the conditions of atomic change was additionally defined by the front line of the hostile power blocks of the world, which cut through Germany herself.

The division of Germany has not been immediately recognizable from the very beginning. The unity of Germany was not yet contested in the "report" on the "important decisions and agreements" of the Potsdam Conference between Stalin, Truman and Attlee on 2 August 1945, even though the setting up of a central German government was postponed for an indefinite period. As, however, the conflict between the Soviet Union and her former western allies sharpened from 1945 onwards, inevitably and step by step the division of Germany west of the Oder-Neisse Line into a western and an eastern part was accomplished. In 1949, two constitutions, recognized for the time being only in the west or the east, came into force: the "Basic Law of the Federal Republic of Germany" ("to bring new order to the life of the state for a transitional period") and the "Constitution of the German Democratic Republic" ("the German people has granted itself this constitution"). The Occupation of both state-like systems was not, however, ended until 1954–5, on the western side by the Treaty of Paris, on the eastern side by a declaration of the Soviet Union, even if thereafter troops of the former enemy powers on both sides remained in the country as allies within the western or eastern defence system. Thus both parts of Germany were fitted into east or west. Since 1945 the unity of Germany has been prevented *de facto* by the division of Europe into two military blocks.

The state of German division created between 1945 and 1955 has not been altered since. The incorporation of the western and the eastern parts of Germany into the western and eastern economic and military systems respectively has been confirmed and extended. Two German armies stand opposite each other, as integrated military forces of NATO on the one hand and the Warsaw Pact on the other. The internal demarcation line was increasingly extended in the course of the fifties and sixties by the German Democratic Republic (GDR) as a fortification in depth, less as a preventive measure against possible attack from the west than to prevent the flight of their own population into the western part of Germany. However, this phenomenon – until 1961 a total of 3.1 million fugitives – went on growing in 1960–61 in spite of this barrier. For at that time the escape route via Berlin was still possible. In order to prevent this western migration that increasingly threatened the stability of the GDR, the government of the GDR – in defiance of the international status of Greater Berlin – constructed in August 1961 a militarily occupied and fortified wall along the zone boundary opposite the three western sectors, which was accepted by the three western powers as a *fait accompli*. Since then, flight has been possible only at the risk of death; after 1961, the phenomenon declined almost completely. Nevertheless, attempts at flight take place continually, sometimes with success, sometimes failing and paid for with death or arrest in the GDR.

The German policy of the two states, with the three western powers on the one hand, and the Soviet Union on the other, has undergone many changes since 1945, without the situation itself fundamentally changing. The Basic Law of the Federal Republic of Germany was produced in 1949 as a provisional constitution. It was to lose its validity on the day "on which a constitution comes into force which is the result of a free decision of the German people" (art. 146), that is, when reunification of the two German states is effected. In the preamble to the Basic Law, the demand is made that the "whole German people" be invited "in free self-determination to consummate the unity and freedom of Germany". This established the central aim of Federal German policy, and it remains unaltered today, irrespective of all the individual modifications by treaty which – increasingly since 1970 – have been directed towards "détente" and "improvement of human relations". In contrast, the GDR has since 1953 increasingly highlighted the fact of the existence of two German states. In the new constitution of 1968, the GDR was contrasted as a "socialist state of the German nation" with the "capitalist" Federal Republic of Germany. The tendency to separation expressed in this was strengthened in 1974 by an alteration to the constitution which deleted all references to the unity of the German nation, especially the statement of intention of reunification in art. 8. In this way the policy of isolation from the west was brought to a head, but the old guideline of GDR policy remained unaltered. Now, as then, it is as follows: (1) Membership by citizens of the GDR of the socialist order, and of the international community of socialist countries, is stronger than the old, nationalist solidarity with those Germans who belong to western "capitalism". (2) Reunification with the western German state can in no circumstances be brought about as a compromise with the western way of life and the liberal democratic political constitution, but only through the take-over of socialism, in the spirit of the "Socialist Unity Party of Germany", in the present Federal Republic of Germany. "Demarcation" is stressed and given precedence again and again in the current situation, but the possibility of reunification by socialist assimilation of the German west into the GDR, seen as unattainable in the near future, is nevertheless not ruled out in spite of changes in the text of the constitution in 1974.

In the sixties the German question, which remained open in international law, was much discussed in diplomatic and journalistic circles both inside and outside Germany. This had an increasing effect in the Federal Republic, even in internal affairs. It is true that the policies of Federal governments, since Chancellor Konrad

Adenauer had established diplomatic relations with the Soviet Union in 1955, had been neither inactive nor rigid, but there was much criticism that by refusing legally to recognize the *status quo* they were blocking détente and marking time in German politics. The Soviet Union and the GDR persistently exerted political pressure following this line of argument.

In 1969 the newly formed coalition government of Willy Brandt and Walter Scheel, which consisted of Social Democrats and Free Democrats, accordingly resolved to bring about by treaties legal settlements which withdrew far enough from the previous legal position of the Federal Government for the way to be opened to better co-operation with the Soviet Union, the GDR and other countries of the socialist block, without the basic demand for German reunification having to be given up as a legal claim.

Thus, with great rapidity, which was described as disadvantageous by critics in the west, there followed a succession of treaties, by which the *de facto* situation in Germany and in eastern central Europe was legalized. In August 1970 the German-Soviet Treaty was signed, in which both sides committed themselves to "respect without limitation the territorial integrity of all states in Europe within their present frontiers" and "to have no territorial claims against anyone nor to make any in the future". This was expressly to apply "inclusive of the Oder-Neisse Line, which forms the western frontier of the People's Republic of Poland and inclusive of the frontier between the Federal Republic of Germany and the German Democratic Republic". On the Federal German side, a "Document on German Unity" by Foreign Minister Scheel expressly declared that these agreements were not in opposition to the political aim of the Federal Republic of Germany "to work towards a position in Europe where the German people once more regain their unity through free self-determination".

The German-Soviet Treaty was followed in December 1970 by a corresponding treaty between the Federal Republic of Germany and the People's Republic of Poland, and a treaty between the four occupying powers of the old German capital, that is the USA, Great Britain, France and the Soviet Union, guaranteeing the status of the western part of Berlin. Finally, in December 1972, a "Treaty on the Principles governing Relations" between the two German states was signed, which was intended to introduce "normal, good-neighbourly relations with each other on the principle of equal rights". The recognition this carries of the GDR as a state within the area of the old German Empire is nevertheless not, as the Federal Republic clearly explained and the Federal Constitutional Court confirmed, the same as recognition in international law, since the treaty partners are two part-states of Germany, and cannot regard each other as foreign countries.

Neither does the final report of the "Conference on European Security and Co-operation" of 1 August 1975, in which the general principle of the "inviolability of frontiers" was strengthened, contradict this Federal German interpretation of the law, since in the final report of the Helsinki Conference the principles of "peaceful change" and of the right to self-determination of peoples, in accordance with art. 1 of the United Nations Convention on Human Rights of 1966, are also expressly mentioned.

Certainly this legal position, which does not exclude German reunification in the future, is disputed by the GDR. In the recent period, it has several times been clearly explained on their side that the German question is no longer "open" and that the formation of two states, who have already greatly diverged as a result of their different political and social constitutions, is irrevocable.

Since the treaties of 1970 to 1972, many negotiations have achieved certain improvements, especially for traffic, journeys, family reunions and the exit of Germans from Poland. Altogether, however, the result in face of the GDR policy of "demarcation", predominant now as before, has remained unsatisfactory up to the present. Criticism of this fact is becoming increasingly loud, even in the GDR. There, too, the Human Rights Movement can no longer be fully denied.

The German question seems to have frozen solid. In the world political line-up of today, there are no signs that a "peaceful change" in the spirit of the right to self-determination can take place in the centre of Europe in the immediate future. The GDR regime has, since 1970, permitted certain improvements in traffic between the German states, but it refuses its citizens, with the exception of the old, permission to travel to the Federal Republic, and even, largely, to have personal contact with the Germans in the west. This fact, together with the Berlin Wall and the fortified line, is an indication that the leadership of party and state in the GDR fear any free exchange of men and ideas. They can only feel relatively safe in isolation, and membership of the block of socialist states under the leadership of the Soviet Union makes their policies inflexible.

However hopeless a unification of both German states in accordance with the principle of self-determination may be at present, it is unthinkable that the maintenance of a rigid policy of isolation and fear of the free west, or continued lack of freedom for their own citizens, should endure in the long term. The German question urgently requires an answer, since the Germans on both sides of the dividing line are making this desire plain, and since in future, just as in the past, the determining and moving forces of the world political system are variable. The German question is open. It cannot be seen in isolation. On the contrary it has taken its place in the global struggle for the achievement of human rights.

SELECT BIBLIOGRAPHY

The following selection includes general surveys, a few titles relating to earlier history and a larger number on the history of the nineteenth and particularly the twentieth century. Most of the titles are of course in German, but where possible English-language editions of German books have been included.

H. Aublin and W. Zorn, eds., *Handbuch der deutschen Wirtschafts- und Sozialgeschichte*, 2 vols. (1971).
G. G. Barraclough, *Factors in German History* (1946).
R. Flenley, *Modern German History* (1953).
B. Gebhardt, *Handbuch der deutschen Geschichte*, ed. by H. Grundmann, 4 vols. (9th ed., 1970–2).
F. Hartung, *Deutsche Verfassungsgeschichte vom 15. Jahrhundert bis zur Gegenwart* (8th ed., 1964).
C. Hinrichs and W. Berges, eds., *Die deutsche Einheit als Problem der europäischen Geschichte* (1960).
H. Holborn, *History of Modern Germany*, 2 vols. (1959–60).
E. R. Huber, *Deutsche Verfassungsgeschichte seit 1789*, 5 vols. (1957–77).
H. Kohn, ed., *German History. Some New German Views* (1954).
G. Mann, *Deutsche Geschichte im 19. und 20. Jahrhundert* (1958).
H. C. Meyer, *Five Images of Germany: Half a Century of American Views on German History* (1960).
H. Plessner, *Die verspätete Nation* (1959).
P. Rassow, ed., *Deutsche Geschichte im Überblick* (1952; 3rd ed., 1973).
H. Simon, *Geschichte der deutschen Nation. Wesen und Wandel des Eigenverständnisses der Deutschen* (1968).
H. Ritter von Srbik, *Deutsche Einheit*, 4 vols. (1935–42).
A. J. P. Taylor, *The Course of German History* (1945).
H. von Treitschke, *History of Germany in the Nineteenth Century*, 5 vols. (1915ff).

K. O. Frh. von Aretin, *Heiliges Römisches Reich 1776–1806. Reichsverfassung und Staatssouveränität*, 2 vols. (1967).

131

G. Barraclough, *The Medieval Empire. Idea and Reality* (1950).
J. Fleckenstein, *Grundlagen und Beginn der deutschen Geschichte* (Deutsche Geschichte, vol. 1, 1974).
B. Möller, *Deutschland im Zeitalter der Reformation* (Deutsche Geschichte, vol. 4, 1977).

W. Conze, ed., *Staat und Gesellschaft im deutschen Vormärz* (1962; 2nd ed., 1970).
R. Koselleck, *Preussen zwischen Reform und Revolution. Allgemeines Landrecht, Verwaltung und soziale Bewegung von 1791–1848* (1967; 2nd ed., 1975).
F. Meinecke, *Weltbürgertum und Nationalstaat. Studien zur Genesis des deutschen Nationalstaats*, 6 vols. (1907–22) (Reprint vol. 5, 1962).
G. Oestreich, *Preussen als historisches Problem. Gesammelte Abhandlungen* (1964).

R. Evans, ed., *Society and Politics in Wilhelmine Germany* (1978).
F. Fischer, *War of Illusions* (1974).
W. von Groote and U. von Gersdorff, eds., *Entscheidung 1866. Der Krieg zwischen Österreich und Preussen* (1966).
A. Hillgruber, *Deutschlands Rolle in der Vorgeschichte der beiden Weltkriege* (1967).
P. Graf Kielmannsegg, *Deutschland und der erste Weltkrieg* (1968).
H. C. Meyer, *Mitteleuropa in German Thought and Action 1815–1945* (1955).
O. Pflanze, *Bismarck and the Development of Germany. The Period of Unification, 1815 to 1871* (1968).
T. Schieder and E. Deuerlein, eds., *Reichsgründung 1870–71. Tatsachen, Kontroversen, Interpretationen* (1970).
T. Schieder, *Das deutsche Kaiserreich als Nationalstaat* (1961).
M. Stürmer, ed., *Das kaiserliche Deutschland. Politik und Gesellschaft 1870–1918* (1970).
H. U. Wehler, *Das deutsche Kaiserreich 1871–1918* (Deutsche Geschichte, vol. 9, 1973).

K. D. Bracher, *Deutschland zwischen Demokratie und Diktatur* (1964).
K. D. Bracher, *Die Auflösung der Weimarer Republik* (1953; 3rd ed., 1960).
K. D. Bracher, *Die deutsche Diktatur. Entstehung, Struktur, Folgen des Nationalsozialismus* (1970).
L. Dehio, *Germany and World Politics in the Twentieth Century* (1960).
K. Hildebrand, *Deutsche Aussenpolitik 1933–45. Kalkül oder Dogma?* (1971).
E. Matthias and R. Morsey, eds., *Das Ende der Parteien 1933* (1960).
F. Meinecke, *The German Catastrophe* (1950).
G. Reitlinger, *The Final Solution* (1953).
G. Ritter, *The German Problem* (1965).

H. Rothfels, *The German Opposition to Hitler* (1947; 2nd ed., 1961).

G. Schultz, *Deutschland seit dem 1. Weltkrieg, 1918–45* (Deutsche Geschichte, vol. 10, 1976).

L. Snyder, *German Nationalism. The Tragedy of a People* (1952).

W. Besson, *Die Aussenpolitik der Bundesrepublik* (1970).

E. Deuerlein, *Deutsche Geschichte der neuesten Zeit von Bismarcks Entlassung bis zur Gegenwart*. Part 3: *Deutschland nach dem 2. Weltkrieg 1945–55* (Handbuch der deutschen Geschichte, ed. by L. Just, 1965).

E. Deuerlein, *Deutschland 1963–70* (1972).

E. Deuerlein, *Die Einheit Deutschlands*. vol. 1: *Die Erörterungen und Entscheidungen der Kriegs- und Nachkriegskonferenzen 1941–49* (2nd ed., 1961).

E. L. Dulles, *One Germany or Two* (1970).

H. Herzfeld, *Berlin in der Weltpolitik 1945–70* (1973).

A. Hillgruber, *Deutsche Geschichte 1945–72* (1974).

R. Löwenthal and H. P. Schwartz, eds., *Die zweite deutsche Republik. Bilanz eines Vierteljahrhunderts* (1973).

H. Merkl, *Die Entstehung der Bundesrepublik Deutschland* (1965).

E. Nolte, *Deutschland und der Kalte Krieg* (1974).

J. Schechtman, *European Population Transfers* (1946).

T. Schieder, ed., *Dokumentation der Vertreibung der Deutschen aus Ost-Mitteleuropa*, 5 vols. (1953–61).

H. P. Schwartz, *Vom Reich zur Bundesrepublik. Deutschland im Widerstreit der aussenpolitischen Konzeptionen in den Jahren der Besatzungsherrschaft 1945–49* (1966).

T. Sharp, *The Wartime Alliance and the Zonal Division of Germany* (1975).

T. Vogelsang, *Das geteilte Deutschland* (1973).

J. Wheeler-Bennet and A. Nichols, *The Semblance of Peace. The Political Settlement after the Second World War* (1972).

A. M. de Zayas, *The Anglo-Americans and the Expulsion of the Germans. Background, Execution, Consequences* (1977).

D. L. Bark, *Agreement on Berlin. A Study of the 1970–77 Quadripartite Negations* (1974).

K. Dochring and G. Ress, *Staats- und völkerrechtliche Aspekte der Berlin-Regelung* (1972).

K. Dochring, W. Kewenig and G. Ress, *Staats- und völkerrechtliche Aspekte der Deutschland- und Ostpolitik* (1971).

E. Deuerlein, *DDR 1945–70. Geschichte und Bestandsaufnahme* (1970).

J. Hacker, *Der Rechtsstatus Deutschlands aus der Sicht der DDR* (1974).

B. Meissner and J. Hacker, *Die Nation in östlicher Sicht* (1977).

H. Weber, *Von der SBZ zur DDR*, 2 vols. (1966–7).

INDEX